ジャパン

JAPAN
EMOJI

エモジ

ED GRIFFITHS

POP PRESS

To
my godson
JACK
&
his sister
ELSIE

contents

Food & drink

Introduction

Welcome to Japanemoji! This book aims to unlock the Japanese power lurking inside all of our smartphones. Emoji have changed the way many of us communicate and, for better or worse, they are now a part of written culture. Beyond their communicative value, emoji have a social dimension too, which reveals that they are Japanese at heart.

The word emoji is Japanese in origin and when written in Japanese script, it comprises three characters:

絵 (e) meaning picture and

文字(moji) meaning character.

If you've ever found yourself scrolling through the emoji repertoire and felt baffled by 🪝 or 無, the answer lies in Japan.

Contained in our phones are many of the building blocks of the culture of Japan – a country beloved and baffling to outsiders in equal measure. This book uses 100 emoji to introduce the reader to Japanese culture from daily encounters to national occasions.

This is the book I wish I'd read when I first lived in Japan, although I wouldn't have missed out on the joy (and occasional embarrassment) of discovering for myself what is contained within its pages. For me, there is more to be gained in trying to piece together an understanding of another society from everyday acts, than there is in ticking off the big-ticket locations in a guidebook.

I hope that reading about the emoji in this book may help you to understand something about which you are curious, to be more adventurous, try new things and – wherever you find yourself in the world – to live a little more Japanese.

The land of the rising sun

Nihon

The Japanese name for Japan is Nihon, written in kanji (see A note about Japanese language) as 日本, 日 meaning 'day' and 本, which has a variety of common meanings but, in this case, represents 'origin' – origin of the day: the land of the rising sun. This name has been employed for Japan since the 7th century CE and, although its precise origins are disputed, the basic meaning undoubtedly hails from a Chinese viewpoint. When the Chinese looked east towards Japan, they would see the dawning sun. The kanji 日本 can also be read Nippon, which is a pronunciation now used in some more formal contexts, such as the names of some companies. Nihon is the country of Japan, nihon-jin (日本人) are Japanese people, and nihon-go (日本語) is the Japanese language.

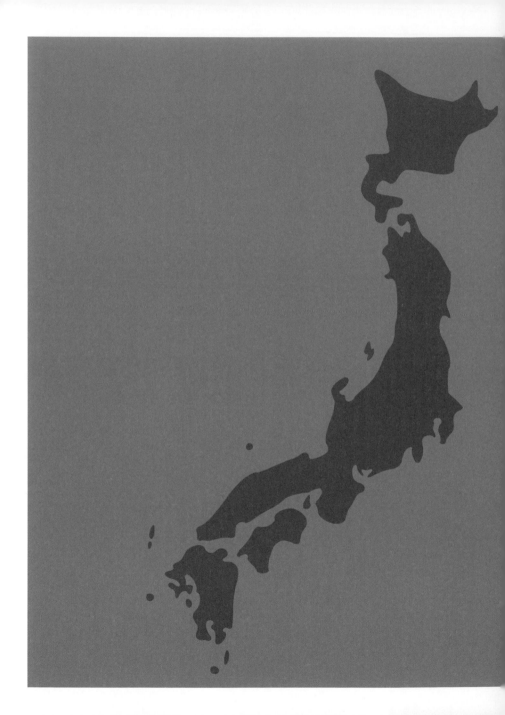

Map of Japan

Nihon chizu

Japan is the only country with the honour of its own map emoji. The country itself consists of many thousands of islands, with four principal large islands. Furthest north is the island of Hokkaidō, with its capital Sapporo. Beneath Hokkaidō lies Honshū, by far the largest of the islands, on which Tokyo, Kyōto, Ōsaka, Hiroshima and many other principal cities are found. Shikoku is the smaller island below western Honshū, separated from it by the Inland (Seto) Sea. The far southwestern island is Kyūshū, with Fukuoka its largest city. Technically part of Kyūshū are the Ryūkyū Islands, of which the many islands of Okinawa (not pictured on the emoji) form part, extending almost as far as Taiwan.

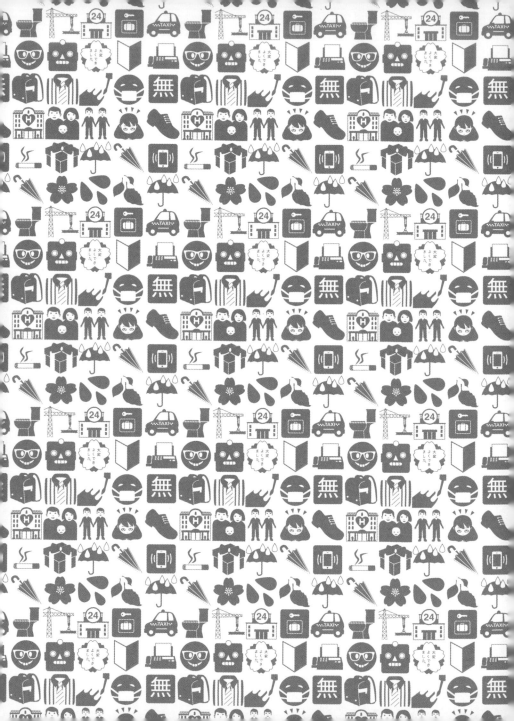

毎日の生活

DAILY LIFE

Rain

ame

Japan has a pronounced rainy season that normally runs from the start of June to the middle of July. The season is known as tsuyu, written in Japanese as 梅雨, or plum rain, as the season roughly coincides with that of the Japanese plum or *ume*.

The beginning and end of the season is officially declared by region and announced on the news or weather forecast. It is generally considered – apart from a reduction in crowds and being the season for beautiful hydrangeas – to be a poor time to visit Japan, as the unpredictable rain is compounded by an increase in humidity. Umbrellas crowd the streets; the sea of umbrellas famously make Shibuya's Scramble crossing a sight to behold in the rain.

Exceptional torrential rain in the 2018 season brought tragedy and extensive flooding to parts of western Japan.

Umbrella

kasa

By far the most common Japanese umbrella is the clear plastic convenience-store version, grabbed hurriedly in a rainy season storm (see opposite). As it is considered impolite to bring a dripping umbrella into a store, there's always somewhere provided outside to leave them. Large stores often have a bagging machine, branded Kasapon, in the entrance way. Put your umbrella into the top and pull towards you to find it emerges neatly bagged up.

The traditional Japanese umbrella, or wagasa (和傘), is made of oiled Japanese paper with many bamboo ribs where the Western equivalent has metal spokes. The straight lines of the shade when it is open provide the classic silhouette of the Japanese umbrella, compared to the dome of the convenience-store equivalent. Unoiled versions are used to shelter from the sun. Another famed type of umbrella with a bullseye pattern of concentric circles on the shade is known as the janomegasa (蛇の目傘), literally serpent's eye umbrella.

Cherry blossom

sakura

Although blossom can be seen in Okinawa as early as January, the main season sweeps up the country from late March in Kyūshū to late April/early May in Hokkaidō. Full bloom in Tokyo, Kyōto and Ōsaka is typically in early April; however, part of the magic of the season lies in its unpredictability. The season is subject to forecasts on television and in newspapers, much like the weather.

Sakura is most often celebrated at hanami (花見 – literally 'flower watching') parties and picnics across the country's parks, with prime spots getting severely overcrowded, and some spots known for more raucous celebrations. You can pick up a picnic mat (known in Japan as a leisure sheet) at a 100-yen shop, and many sakura-watching spots serve themed drinks and sweets. Retailers go into overdrive around this time, with sakura lattes, sparkling wine, cakes and plenty more on offer. Where sakura indicates a taste, it's often a slightly floral cherry flavour or, more traditionally, the salt-pickled buds or leaves of the tree, which are wrapped around sweet and sticky sakura mochi.

The plum blossom season is also celebrated in Tokyo between February and March at plum festivals (梅まつり, ume matsuri), which herald the changing season with a quieter but no less lovely, feel.

Sweat

ase

汗

A historical lack of central heating in Japan means that air-conditioning units that both cool and warm are standard in most Japanese homes (turning on the air con in winter means turning on the heating), except in northern Japan, and provide considerable relief from the summer heat.

Moving around is, however, an undeniably sweaty business in hotter months. It's perfectly polite – in fact, desirable – to mop your brow with a small towel carried for the purpose. These vary depending on the extent to which they're required, from a dainty dab, to full mop-down by a stressed salaryman running for the train. Traditional Japanese towels known as tenugui make affordable, attractive and easy-to-pack souvenirs.

Look out for the phenomenally popular Japanese rehydration drink Pocari Sweat, which also has a (deserved) cult following as a hangover cure.

Autumn leaves

kōyō

紅
葉

The changing colour of the autumn leaves sweeps southward down the country in the reverse direction to the cherry blossom, beginning on the north island Hokkaidō in late September. It is a hardier affair than sakura blossom, with a longer-lasting and slightly more predictable season, though it is said that the leaves won't start to turn until the temperature drops to 5–7°C.

The Japanese for the season, 紅葉, represents the colour crimson in the first character and the word for leaf in the second, and has two alternate readings: kōyō or momiji. Momiji often refers more specifically to the Japanese maple, or *acer palmatum*, which is thought of as the king of the fall and emblematic of the season as a whole. Just as viewing the blossom is known as hanami, viewing the changing leaves is known as momijigari (紅葉狩り).

The Japanese often discover their favoured spots over time, but for first-timers, Kyōto draws the crowds, and Mt Takao and Nikkō (see Tengu and Three Wise Monkeys) are popular day trips from Tokyo. The season also represents a great opportunity for a hike into the lesser known Japanese countryside. Approximate calendars of the timings for kōyō can be found online.

Yen

en

The English language word 'yen' represents a much older pronunciation of the Japanese word, which was imported and used by early missionaries and lexicographers. The Japanese pronunciation has long since become 'en'. The kanji 円 and the currency sign ¥ are used interchangeably.

The use of cash still prevails in Japan, but credit cards are accepted in all major shops and the use of prepaid cards, known as IC cards ('integrated circuit' for the curious), is extremely prevalent. The Suica and Pasmo cards (interchangeable in the Tokyo area, with coverage varying outside of the capital) are among the most common and available for purchase from any train station. They can be used to pay at vending machines (touch once before selecting the product, and once after), in some taxis, and in stores wherever you see their logos.

The 100-en shop (100円ショップ, hyaku-en shoppu) is a fixture of the Japanese High Street – Daiso and Seria are two of the most common. The 100-yen shop is considered one of the usual places to stock up on household goods, cleaning products and DIY materials in Japan. Bargain items that make good souvenirs are to be found in tableware, chopsticks, bento-box accessories, onigiri moulds, fans, and slippers that clean the floor with their undersides. If you're unsure where to buy an everyday item in Japan, try the Don Quijote (known universally as the Donki), which is a discount store rather than a 100-yen shop.

Taxi

takushī

The taxi emoji doesn't do justice to the wonderful old-school glamour of the Japanese taxi. In a country that is at best uncomfortable with the gig economy, Uber has only a tiny presence in Tokyo and none at all outside of the capital; so if you're looking to travel in style, it's best to hail on the street.

The most commonly seen type is the, usually splendidly gleaming, Toyota Comfort, although electric hybrid models are also encountered. Back seats are invariably spotlessly clean and covered in a white fabric; drivers often also wear white gloves. Perhaps most famously of all, there's no need for you to open the back left door. The driver will operate it for you from the front of the cab on entering and exiting the taxi... It's the little things.

Taxis are not cheap, although the minimum fare in Tokyo was recently lowered. Drivers' levels of English naturally vary. Some will offer a translation sheet to which you can point. The driver's desire to provide a good service can often lead to a lot of concerned checking that they have correctly understood your request.

Taxis display their status on an electronic panel in the windscreen. The sign for an available cab is 空車 (kūsha) and is, confusingly, always displayed in red.

Payment is quite often accepted by IC card (see opposite), but less often by credit card.

Toilet

toire

ト
イ
レ

The Japanese pronunciation of toilet is 'toi-lé', as if it has a silent t. Bathrooms are sometimes indicated as o-tearai (お手洗い). To ask for directions, it is simply 'toire wa, doko des(u) ka'; or 'Sumimasen [excuse me], toire wa?' will do the trick.

The yin to the yang of the Space Age toilets, for which Japan is famed, is found in the old-fashioned squat toilets still in use in some stations, parks and rural areas; although there's often a choice of a 'Western' toilet, too. The squat toilets have a hood, this is the direction in which you face.

The bidet toilets, commonly known as washlets, are everywhere in Japan, in homes and public toilets alike. Buttons are sometimes labelled in English, too, although it is by no means uncommon to find Japanese characters only on control panels.

The flush button is marked 大 for a long flush, 小 for short. If you don't fancy taking your chances guessing the wash functions by the pictures alone, then it's おしり (oshiri) for behind, ビデ (bide) for bidet for women. Stop is 止.

Finding these super-efficient loos impossibly funny or mortifying is slightly counter-cultural in a country where they have become the norm. No need to be embarrassed. Push the button.

Construction

kōji

The Japanese take the efficiency of construction work seriously and many roadworks are undertaken at night to reduce disruption to traffic flow during the day.

Construction workers (particularly those who work at heights) sport baggy trousers known as tobi-zubon, derived from knickerbockers, which to the unadjusted eye can look more catwalk than construction site, and indeed have a fashion following.

Hello Kitty road barriers, occasionally seen during construction work, are generally considered to be at the far reaches of kawaii culture.

Convenience store
konbini

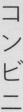

The 24-hour convenience store is an essential part of everyday life in Japan. The Japanese often use the word 'convenient' to describe daily life in their country; nothing exemplifies this better than the humble konbini. You may never need to buy suit deodorant at 3am, but it's reassuring to know the option is there.

The konbini's stock proudly changes with the season, with till-point oden (see Oden) a winter staple, while in summer iced coffee is particularly popular. Take a sealed cup of ice from the freezer, pay at the till and then fill at the coffee machines at the front of the store. Seasonal desserts in the chiller cabinet can provide particularly delicious and surprising treats.

Branches of Family Mart include a small section of Muji essentials, while 7-Eleven cashpoints are a safe bet for withdrawals using international cards. Photocopying and printing are also available (see Further Resources) and many konbini have a bathroom for customer use.

Coin locker

koinrokkā

Japan is phenomenally well equipped with left-luggage lockers at stations, department stores and public attractions. It's worth bearing these safe and efficient amenities in mind before lugging heavy bags or shopping around a city.

The train-station coin locker was immortalised in Japanese pop culture in the 1980 novel *Coin Locker Babies* by Ryū Murakami, Japan's lesser-known Murakami, about the subsequent lives of two baby brothers found abandoned in a Tokyo coin locker.

The words 'coin locker' typify the many loan words from other languages into Japanese, which are sometimes easy to understand, though at the same time not quite natural in English. English words that have come into Japanese without having the equivalent meaning in English are known as wasei eigo – examples include sheamēto ('sharemate' for roommate) and gasorin sutando ('gasoline stand' for gas station). Not all loan words come from English, however. A part-time job in Japan is universally known as an arubaito (or baito for short), which derives from the German for work, Arbeit.

Fax machine

fakkusu

フ
ァ
ッ
ク
ス

Anyone expecting wall-to-wall neon and robot interaction in Japan has a shock in store. The country manages an extraordinary balancing act between high and low tech. Items that achieved global reach in the tech boom of the '80s and '90s have found in Japan a last bastion of popularity. Nothing embodies this more than the persistent endurance of the fax machine.

Surveys undertaken within the past decade have estimated that between 45% and 60% of Japanese homes still own one and they are commonly found in business hotel rooms. The humble fax is very often given as a communication option with companies such as Japan Post for mail re-delivery, banks and the national broadcaster, NHK. Indeed, it is still possible to fax orders through to popular restaurants for delivery. Some of the fax's popularity can be explained by technology's delay with dealing with the complex Japanese writing system but the fax's deep roots point also to the country's culture of handwritten communication and the formal paper trail in business.

Nerd

otaku

オタク

Using the word otaku as a translation for nerd is a complex and sensitive issue. While many people in and outside Japan increasingly self-identify as otaku, within Japan the word is emerging from a complex history with multiple negative connotations to be used to celebrate the fans, enthusiasts and obsessives with a passion for anything from anime, games and manga to trains and history.

Whatever the terminology used, for many, Japan represents geek heaven, with its centre found in the Electric Town in Tokyo suburb Akihabara (often shortened to Akiba). Many visitors head to its shops and maid and cosplay cafés to indulge their inner otaku. Though guidebooks often name Takeshita-dōri in Harajuku as the best street to spot cosplay and other Japanese crazes, the scene has unsurprisingly moved on, and Takeshita-dōri is now the best place for a scrum of tourists and the overwhelming smell of sugar from the outrageous crepes sold there filled with ice cream, brownies, whipped cream or even an entire slice of cheesecake.

Robot

robotto

ロ
ボ
ッ
ト

Those who come to Japan in search of a robot future will find much of interest. Indeed, Tokyo's Bladerunner skyline in high-rise districts like Shinjuku immediately brings to mind the future we were always promised. While no robot has broken through to conquer the general market, Pepper, the humanoid robot made by the robotics arm of mobile-phone company Softbank, is perhaps the most visible in Japan. According to Softbank, he is 'kindly, endearing and surprising', though 'surprising' may not be top of everyone's list of desirable qualities in a robot.

Pepper is famed for his ability to read human emotions, which will doubtless be a necessary quality in the robots who staff Japan's robot-run Henn-na hotels ('Strange Hotels'). The branch in Maihama, in Chiba prefecture, near Tokyo Disneyland, houses 140 robots for 100 rooms with an all-robot reception desk, robot porters and in-room assistant robots called Tapia. The original Henn-na Hotel is located in Nagasaki prefecture, with more in the pipeline.

Tech fans looking for a more sensory experience are catered for in a new virtual-reality centre called VR Land in Tokyo's Shibuya.

Visitors arriving at Tokyo's Haneda Airport for the 2020 Olympics can be expected to be greeted by seven new robots, including a multi-lingual humanoid called Cinnamon, who can help with directions.

White flower
taihen yoku dekimashita

大
変
よ
く
で
き
ま
し
た

This emoji depicts stamp of approval awarded by teachers for good work. The above wording is contained within a blossom-flower symbol and loosely translates as 'very well done', or 'you did well'. Stamps and stickers are much used in Japanese education and make good souvenirs. A wide selection is available in the stationery section of any department store.

Beginners' mark

shoshinsha māku

初
心
者
マ
ー
ク

Newly qualified Japanese drivers have to display the shoshinasha mark, also known as the wakaba (若葉, young leaf) mark, on their car for a year after passing a driving test. It is sometimes used more generally to denote beginner status. At the other end of the spectrum, 高齢者マーク, the kōreisha mark, is used to indicate an elderly driver, and is optional for anyone over 70 or whose age may inhibit their driving skills, and compulsory from the age of 75.

The previous kōreisha mark was often known as the autumn leaf, or fallen leaf, in contrast to the young shoots suggested by the wakaba mark. The symbolism was considered potentially offensive to the elderly and in 2011 it was replaced with an icon with colours of all the seasons, light and dark green, orange and yellow. Overseas fans of JDM (Japanese Domestic Market) cars have confusingly appropriated the beginner mark shape, with the yellow and green colours often replaced with the flag of their country.

Free

mu-

This Chinese character (kanji – see A Note on Written Japanese) is the first character in the Japanese word muryō (無料) meaning free of charge. However, it is seen on shopping streets across the world signifying a different kind of free – in the famously label free stores Muji, or mu-jirushi-ryō-hin (無印良品, 'brand-free quality goods'). The range started out as the own-brand line of a supermarket chain and has grown into a global anti-brand shopping phenomenon. The larger Japanese branches are worth searching out for the wide range of packaged convenience foods and snacks, which make good souvenirs, and in some stores customers can desecrate the unbranded goods by personalising them with stamps. The Yurakuchō flagship store in Tokyo holds a Meal Muji café and an assembled example of the Muji Hut (koya, 小屋), which may yet provide the flat-pack key to housing of the future, all yours for 3 million yen, though regrettably a plot of Japanese land does not come included.

School backpack

randoseru

ランドセル

The distinctive Japanese school backpack with one firm flat side is known as the randoseru, from an outdated Dutch word for a rucksack 'ransel'. They are notorious for being much more expensive that the average schoolbag, with the top made-in-Japan models sold for the equivalent of hundreds of dollars. The price tag is explained by their expected longevity – a schoolchild is intended to keep this bag for all 6 years of elementary school. They are sized accordingly and younger-age school children can often be seen walking determinedly along the street with their oversize cargo looking as though it may topple them. The bags used to be available only in red for girls and black for boys though a more diverse colour choice is now available. The bags have become unlikely fashion icons; the actor Zooey Deschanel confused the Japanese when she was photographed sporting this icon of infancy, though Japanese hipsters have also been known to appropriate them into their own style.

Tie

nekutai

ネクタイ

The tie (always necktie in Japanese English) in Japan, has in recent years become emblematic of a tension between environmental concerns and the uniformly smart dress expected of the Japanese office worker. A 2005 campaign known as Cool Biz, spearheaded by the then Environment Minister Yuriko Koike, encouraged male government workers to ditch the jacket and tie and women to dress in lighter clothing to reduce the need for air conditioning. The campaign has become a fixture of the stifling Japanese summer and has been variously adopted in the private sector as well, though there has been controversy over the appropriateness of the 28°C limit set as the recommended temperature for A/C units. Cool Biz became Super Cool Biz following the nuclear accident caused by the devastating Tōhoku earthquake and tsunami of March 2011 when power shortages made the need to conserve electricity more pressing.

Beauty

byūtī

ビューティー

The beauty industry in Asia is big business and Japan leads the way, globally, in per capita spending. The bewildering array of beauty products on display in everyday drugstores like Matsumoto Kiyoshi pay testament to this and make these seemingly workaday shops tourist destinations in their own right. The Japanese tendency towards minimal and natural make-up puts skincare top of the agenda, with the aim of mochi hada, skin like the pillowy soft rice-flour sweets called mochi. Restaurants can be found specialising in soups and stews with naturally collagen-rich ingredients such as pig's feet. Collagen can also be found added to vitamin drinks found in the small vitamin-drinks fridge in every convenience store. Also sold among these little bottles of goodness is the preventative hangover cure Hepalyse (ヘパリーゼ, heparīze).

Mask

masuku

マスク

In a country with a phenomenal work ethic and sense of duty to one's company, and where commuters pack into trains like sardines, one of the common uses of masks is to prevent yourself getting sick.

However, the circumstances in which it's almost obligatory to wear a mask is if you yourself are sick and (inevitably) come to work anyway. In that case, a mask must be worn out of respect for others.

While the popularity of these masks in China is caused by the extreme pollution in many cities, this is a more secondary reason in Japan. Japan's significant hayfever season also causes a surge in their use. Some Japanese women also report the helpfulness of masks on 'no make-up days', while shy people can find masks easier to retreat behind. Masks are available at every convenience store, with a larger range, including medicated masks, available in drugstores such as Matsumoto Kiyoshi.

Shoes

kutsu

靴

Japanese people remove shoes before entering their home, in a hallway or small area known as the genkan. This is absolutely universal and applies despite the level to which housing styles have become more Westernised in recent years. A small step or change in level usually indicates the threshold between the two.

Cleanliness is the primary explanation of the custom, though the genkan also has a psychological dimension, separating the world of outside (and work) from the domestic inside. This is reflected also in the couplet (Tadaima/O-kaeri, 'I'm back'/ 'Welcome home') used daily to welcome family members back to the home.

Other places where shoes are removed are in Izakaya (see Izakaya lantern) and Japanese restaurants with seating on the traditional zashiki (tatami mat) floor. In restaurants where shoes are removed, slippers or sandals are provided at the entrance to, or just inside, the bathroom. These are for use in the bathroom only. Shoes are also removed before entering shrines and temples, as well as any onsen, or changing room (including those in clothes shops).

Love hotel

rabu hoteru

ラ
ブ
ホ
テ
ル

From seedier origins, love hotels gained a more mainstream acceptance born from simple practicalities. Around the 1960s, with the traditional Japanese home occupied by generations of the same family and with paper-thin walls, couples began looking for spaces to go for a bit of 'peace and quiet'.

More recently, love hotels have begun marketing themselves towards women, who are said to make up to 90% of love-hotel bookings. The highest concentrations in Tokyo are found on Shibuya's famous Love Hotel Hill and in Shinjuku's Kabuki-chō. A reported 1.37 million people a day visit the love hotels… So, choose wisely, select a 'rest' or an overnight 'stay' and make (out) like the Japanese.

Family
(go-)kazoku

The concept of family in Japan is central to society and the idea of respect within and towards the family is of high importance.

Different words are used if talking about someone else's family rather than your own, employing the honorific -san (which is never used about your own family, or yourself). The translation go-kazoku above uses the honorific prefix go- only when talking about or enquiring after someone else's family.

For the generations immediately after the Second World War, the stereotype of the father as breadwinner and the mother as nurturer persisted, though the slow modernisation of this picture can also be discerned. One area where the statistics speak for themselves is in the country's declining birth rate; the number of children born in Japan in 2017 dropped for the first time below 1 million. Work ethic, gender equality and the importance placed on company productivity all play their part in the declining population. Perhaps the decline, along with the desertion of parts of the Japanese countryside, may be evened out by the automation of workforces and an evolving desire to escape overcrowded and expensive cities. These are, however, big ifs, and undoubtedly the declining population would be cited by many Japanese people as one of the country's greatest worries.

Gay culture

gei bunka

ゲイ文化

Six regional governments in Japan, including the Shibuya and Setagaya wards in Tokyo, now issue same-sex partnership certificates with an equivalent standing to marriage certificates, which represents a platform for improvement in a country where one of the greatest issues facing LGBT society is the lack of visibility.

LGBT issues have rarely figured in high profile political debates and there are few gay figures in public life. The theme of Tokyo's Rainbow Pride in 2017, however, was change and there do seem to be signs that the country *is* slowly changing. Most encouragingly, opinions polls show support for equal marriage, with overwhelming support from the younger generation.

The city of Ōsaka recently recognised a same-sex couple as foster parents for the first time. Ōsaka has a famously lively gay scene, focused in an area called Dōyama, and Tokyo's most famous gay district is Shinjuku's 2-Chome (Ni-chome).

Bow
O-jigi

お
辞
儀

The etiquette of bowing in Japan sometimes gives rise to worry for visitors to the country. Perhaps as an act of non-linguistic communication, it should feel easier to conquer than the language barrier; yet the complexity and unfamiliarity of the situation proves otherwise.

The bad news is that it is undeniably complicated, to the extent that Japanese companies sometimes train their employees to bow properly. The good news is that Japanese people don't generally expect foreigners to understand the detailed rules. On non-business trips, the vast majority of visitors are bowed to as customers, where the only reciprocity needed is a smile and a slight bow of the head. Mastery of basic spoken greetings will, however, be appreciated. In a situation that does appear to call for bowing, remember to stop and not rush, a 30-degree bow with a straight back would serve most purposes. In more complex business situations, it is advisable to read about the customs in more detail or seek advice from your hosts.

The etiquette of exchanging business cards respectfully with both hands is important, keeping the card visible rather than pocketing it, and not writing on it. The Japanese order in which an introduction is made in business – company name first, then department, then name, tells you much about the importance of the company over the individual in traditional Japanese business.

Manner mode

manāmōdo

マ
ナ
ー
モ
ー
ド

Manner mode is the name given to switching your phone to silent in Japan (see Coin Locker for further discussion of Japanese English). The phrase itself is telling of the importance of good manners across Japan – this extends to switching your phone to silent on all public transport; talking on the phone is also considered impolite. The promotion of silence makes the experience of travelling on crowded Japanese commuter transport more bearable but is also emblematic of the general importance of quietness in Japanese culture, particularly given the close proximity in which people often live to their neighbours. If Japanese etiquette can sometimes seem complex and overwhelming, dialling it down a notch is one area that is easy to get right.

Japanese mobile phones are, however, louder than others in one respect – by law, the 'shutter' sound produced by taking a photo cannot be turned to silent. This is to prevent phone cameras being used to invade privacy or for voyeuristic purposes.

Cigarette

tabako

た
ば
こ

Japan has lagged behind the WHO conventions on the subject of smoking and strong pro-smoking groups among politicians in government have caused many proposals to stall. Ahead of the 2020 Olympic and Paralympic Games, legislation was passed banning smoking in most public buildings, but with provisions for smaller establishments to allow smoking and for others to install smoking rooms.

Izakaya chains (see Izakaya lantern) are among the opponents to any public bans and the izakaya and other small locally frequented restaurants are certainly places where smoking culture is still firmly knitted into the fabric of Japanese culture. In large cities, it is often illegal, and impolite, to smoke walking along the street, and smoking areas, particularly outside stations, are often crowded. The legal age at which you can buy cigarettes in Japan is 20, currently still the legal age of adulthood in Japan, and, consequently, the same for alcohol. Street cigarette vending machines now require an identity card to restrict their use by minors.

Gift

okurimono

贈
り
物

Gift-giving is important in Japanese culture and an essential when visiting the home of a Japanese person. In certain, often business, situations, etiquette around price and value comes into play (see Fruit), but small gifts and tokens of kindness are also commonly exchanged when someone has helped you, or when asking for a favour. The tradition of giving of omiyage (お土産) when translated as 'souvenir-giving' can sound slightly dated, but the custom is omnipresent in Japanese life and simply involves buying a gift (often of a local food) to give to family, friends or colleagues when you return from a trip. Boxed omiyage are impossible to miss at train stations or airports, especially in a region with a famed speciality. The fine gesture of omiyage-giving reflects Japanese pride in the country's produce and passion for domestic travel.

When buying an item in Japan, the sales assistant will often ask if it is a gift and wrap accordingly; Japanese shop-wrapping is often in a league of its own. The Japanese tradition when giving a gift of using wrapping fabric known as furoshiki (風呂敷), which belongs to and is retained by the present-giver rather than -receiver, has declined over time, though it is now having a resurgence of interest for its eco credentials, aesthetic beauty and practical versatility as an everyday bag or bento transporter.

文化

CULTURE

化

Calendar

karendā

カ
レ
ン
ダ
ー

Japan uses the Gregorian calendar in parallel with a number of other systems, the most notable of which is the common use of the year of the Emperor's reign. The Gregorian date is given in the order year-month-day, each followed by their kanji, so 17 July 2019 reads 2019年7月17日. Use of the imperial-era dating system is standard on formal documents. The era of Emperor Akihito is known as Heisei, with 2018 being Heisei 30 (平成30年), for example, and a new era will begin with the abdication of the Emperor Akihito in favour of his son Crown Prince Naruhito.

Year 1 of an imperial era runs from the date of the emperor's accession until 31 December of that year, with Year 2 running from 1 January. Showa, the era of the Emperor Hirohito, was the longest reign of any emperor, until his death on 7 January 1989. The first 7 days of 1989 were categorised as Showa 64; Heisei 1 began on 8 January of the same year.

Kimono

kimono

着
物

The prosaic meaning of the word kimono ('thing to be worn') belies the intricate beauty of a garment that has captured imaginations across the world. Today, kimono are most commonly worn by men and women on formal occasions such as the Coming of Age ceremony or weddings. Styles of kimono, particularly for women, vary considerably, the long-sleeved furisode, for example, is worn only by unmarried women. The yukata is a more informal, often cotton, version of the garment worn in summer by men and women, and often worn for the fireworks displays that are a staple of the Japanese summer.

The expense and relative impracticality of the kimono has seen a marked decline in their regular wear; though it is not completely uncommon to see women of an older generation in Japan dressed in the kimono as part of their daily wear. The promotion of kimono rental opportunities to tourists is a more common sight. The wearing of kimono by non-Japanese people has become a flashpoint for the argument about 'cultural appropriation' in recent years. It is a complex argument, though one no doubt more easily mitigated by a measure of self-awareness and sensitivity. In any event, it's clear that the influence of the kimono spread long ago beyond Japanese shores. Recent easy-to-wear yukata sold in Japan by UNIQLO have shown an appetite for a more relaxed and affordable traditional dress in the marketplace.

Shrine

jinja

神
社

Shintō (神道) is the ancient original religion of Japan, and as old as the country itself. The word literally means the 'way of the gods' and it denotes the Japanese way of life, and a faith in the divinity of kami (神) often translated as 'gods', for the lack of a true English equivalent. There is no single god in Shintō, nor a founder, or a holy book.

According to the Shintō faith, the country of Japan was created by a male and a female kami but the divinity of kami can be seen in human beings and in nature: in mountains, valleys, oceans, or in particular trees or rocks that inspire awe. There is a parallel reverence for the natural spiritual beauty of Japan and for the contribution of the country's ancestors.

There are approximately 80,000 shrines in the country dedicated to the Shintō faith. The entry to a shrine is marked by the gates ('torii' 鳥居) depicted in the emoji, which denote that the space within is sacred. Many visitors to Japan visit Tokyo's Meiji Shrine (明治神宮 Meiji jingū) dedicated to the divine souls of the Emperor Meiji and his wife Empress Shōken, and 100,000 trees were donated from across Japan and across the world in their memory. Nearly 100 years later, the planned eternal forest is an extraordinary and beautiful feature of central Tokyo. Outside of the capital, the floating torii of Itsukushima Shrine in Hiroshima Prefecture is perhaps one of Japan's most famous gateways to a shrine.

Buddism is commonly practised (at temples rather than shrines) by many Japanese people, in parallel with Shintō.

Three wise monkeys

sanzaru

The mountain town of Nikkō and its sites of worship, which are relatively easily accessible from Tokyo, make a popular day or overnight trip. Nikkō is noted for its stunning autumn-leaf season (see Autumn leaves), but its most celebrated attraction lies in the 17th-century Shinto shrine of Tosho-gū. Three monkeys on a frieze within the stables for the shrine's sacred horses are the oldest known representation of the axiom of 'see no evil, hear no evil, speak no evil'. Monkeys are traditionally regarded as guardians of horses and this is their primary purpose here.

The shrine is a UNESCO World Heritage Site, and the sanzaru were restored in March 2017.

Izakaya lantern
akachōchin

赤
提
灯

These red lanterns hang outside Japan's izakayas. The word izakaya (居酒屋) is often equated to 'pub', which captures the sense that they are a place to go to drink and socialise. But food also plays an important part in the experience, without the formality of an ordered full meal. Food is shared – it is common to serve your friends first and doing so captures the feeling of sharing in the food. Japanese snack dishes like edamame and fried chicken (karaage) sit with any variety of other menu choices such as sashimi, Korean-inspired dishes or Western snacks like potato fries and Japan-style potato salad and pizza. The structure is loose and convivial. Popular drinks include beer, nihonshu (see Sake), shōchū, highball cocktails, a lethal variant of which is known as chū-hai when made with shōchū, and Westernised cocktails such as the popular lemon sour.

All-you-can-eat (tabehōdai, 食べ放題) and all-you-can-drink (nomihōdai, 飲み放題) timed deals are often available and represent good value, among other things. An evening in an izakaya is an essential experience. Although izakayas can be big and spread across multiple floors, reservations are a good idea for large parties or busy times such as Friday nights.

Wind chimes

fūrin

Wind chimes gained popularity in Japan through the Buddhist belief that they would drive away evil spirits. The introduction of glass to Japan during the late Edo period provided an alternative to bronze, which had kept them exclusively for the very wealthy. The sound is a historical reminder of the period. The use of wind chimes is particularly associated with the stiflingly humid Japanese summer, when, in a cross-sensory but perhaps believable feat, their sound is believed to offer respite from the heat. Think cool thoughts.

Tengu

tengu

天
狗

The tengu is a class of Japanese supernatural monster known as yōkai. Parallel traditions depict the tengu either as an avian creature with a beak and wings, or as the anthropomorphic long-nosed demon seen in the emoji, sometimes known as daitengu (big tengu).

The tengu's interpretation has varied wildly throughout history from enemies of Buddhism and distracters of those on the path to enlightenment, to kidnappers of children, or benevolent kami (see Shrine) acting as guardians of nature. Despite the considerable variation in their mythology, tengu are widely believed to dwell in mountains. Mt. Takao makes a popular hiking day trip from Tokyo, where notable tengu statues can be seen at its Yakuō-in temple, along with the extraordinary Octopus Cedar tree, whose roots curled back on themselves like an octopus's tentacles to make way for the tengu as they built a path to the summit.

Namahage

namahage

なまはげ

The namahage is the name of the demon who commonly appears in a New Year ritual in the city of Oga in Akita Prefecture. The namahage appear at New Year (traditionally on the 15th day of the first lunar month of the year, known as Little New Year), but now more commonly on December 31st with the role played by young men dressed in the masks, straw costumes and wielding pretend carving knives. Calling from house to house, they hunt out the lazy, frightening children in the process, and are appeased with gifts of sake and mochi (soft rice flour sweets).

Traditionally, the namahage's target was all lazy people and one of their traditional cries still pertains to using their knives to peel blisters obtained by those who sit constantly around the fire. The namahage is now used as an archetypal warning to lazy children, comparable to a terrifying Santa Claus. Though the namahage's origins and its rituals are distinct, the imagery of its face resembles the generic Japanese oni (devil or ogre).

Kadomatsu

kadomatsu

門
松

The kadomatsu (literally 'gate pine') is emblematic of New Year (o-shōgatsu, お正月) in Japan and are placed outside front doors to welcome in Toshigami-sama, the kami (see Shrine) who visit at New Year. Kadomatsu vary in size, but can be really quite substantial. Though the three-tier bamboo shoots at first sight can dominate visually, it is the pine for which they are named. Symbolism features heavily in the uprightness of the bamboo, the evergreen longevity of the pine and, often, plum flowers, the first blossom to appear after the winter.

The kadomatsu must not be placed outside during the period 29–31 December. The 29th is considered an unlucky day and decorating on the 31st is known as ichiyakazari (one night decoration) and shows a lack of respect in having failed to take time to prepare. The 28th, therefore, is often considered the best day; with 7 January often used as the day to take them down.

The three heights of the bamboo shoots, in common with a central principle of ikebana (the Japanese art of arranging flowers), can be interpreted as representing heaven (the highest), man (the middle) and earth (the lowest).

Japanese dolls
hina ningyō

雛
人
形

These dolls, which are said to represent members of the Imperial Family, either a prince and princess, or emperor and empress, are used to celebrate what's known as Dolls' Day (hina matsuri, 雛祭り) on 3 March, which has been adopted as National Girls' Day.

A few days before the festival, families with daughters set up these dolls and others around them on special red tiered stands called hinadan. Many of these are prized family heirlooms. Because the festival coincides with peach-blossom season, pink colours and food are used to celebrate.

The festival has been seen as a valuable day to celebrate girls in a society often thought of as male-dominated. There are drives to make the day a celebration of Japanese adult women and girls alike, and to ensure that Children's Day (see Carp streamer) is now a truly unisex celebration.

Carp streamer

koi nobori

鯉のぼり

Carp streamers are displayed in Japan to celebrate Children's Day (kodomo no hi, こどもの日) on 5 May, the last in the series of national holidays that form Golden Week, the longest and busiest holiday period of the year. The amount of domestic tourism undertaken by the Japanese during Golden Week pushes prices through the roof and is best avoided by the traveller who can afford to plan dates accordingly.

Carp streamers are flown in the weeks before Children's Day to honour children for their individual talents and to wish them happiness. The carp is chosen for its symbolic trait of determination in swimming upstream and represents the desire for Japanese children to grow into strong adults. For the latest incarnation of Children's Day, which has replaced the celebration for Boys' Day on the same date, a large black carp represents the family's father, a red carp the mother, with blue, green, purple or orange carp for as many children as the family has, in decreasing sizes.

Star festival
Tanabata

Tanabata is a festival celebrated in summer with its basis in a legend told to all Japanese children: the story concerns the heavenly princess Orihime, daughter of the deity Tentei, who spends long days weaving beautiful cloth for her father. Lonely and wishing to fall in love, she is introduced to the cowherd Hikoboshi. Their subsequent love causes them to neglect their duty and angers Tentei, who separates them by the Milky Way. Desperate at her loss, Orihime begs her father, who subsequently allows the lovers to meet on one day a year – the seventh day of the seventh (lunar) month – provided the weather is clear. If it rains on Tanabata, the lovers must wait another year to be reunited.

The festival is celebrated on different days according the local tradition, from 7 July, to the famous celebrations in Sendai between 6–8 August, or a shifting day in August according to the Japanese lunar calendar.

Wishes for the future are written on paper strips known as tanzaku and tied to specially designated bamboo trees along with colourful paper streamers, which represent Orihime's woven fabric.

お月見

Moon viewing

o-tsukimi

Tsukimi is an autumn festival held to celebrate the clear and beautiful September moon, with the full moon celebrated on a changing day each year, defined as the 15th day of the 8th lunar month. It is a quiet celebration, with decorative arrangements of pampas grass and the chewy rice-flour dumplings known as dango (see Dango) piled in a pyramid often arranged at a small altar, as seen in the emoji. Dango are often bright and sticky affairs, but tsukimi dango are plain and pure white in honour of the moon. Other autumn foods such as chestnuts or sweet potato are often served.

Mount Fuji
Fuji-san

There are few places more deeply embedded in the Japanese consciousness than Mt Fuji. The country's highest mountain, standing at 3,776 metres, with its near-perfect symmetry and relative proximity to the capital, has inspired countless artists, photographers, climbers and visitors.

As Fuji-san is snow-capped for much of the year, the climbing season is short and runs from early July to early September and is a relatively serious undertaking. A more accessible attraction is the twice-yearly phenomenon of Diamond Fuji, when sunrise and sunset align perfectly with the peak of the mountain. Dates vary by year and according to viewing location but are usually in October/November and late January/February. On a clear day, Diamond Fuji can be seen from Tokyo but keen photographers and Fuji worshippers should travel closer to take full advantage.

A common (and charming) misconception is that the Japanese Fuji-san contains the same 'san' used as a term of respect when added to someone's name (Mr/Ms/Mrs Fuji). In fact, this is one of the many examples of identical sounds in Japanese having different meanings and in this case 'san' is simply the Chinese reading of the kanji for mountain (山).

Bullet train

shinkansen

新
幹
線

Japan's high-speed train network is justifiably admired throughout the world. Sleek, precise, safe, comfortable and with speeds of up to 320km/h, like all good trains they inspire a significant fan base, with new lines and trains booking out in record times. There are seven main bullet train lines (some with off-shoots), which run the length and breadth of Honshū, and also connect to Kyūshū and to Hakodate on the southern tip of Hokkaidō (see Map of Japan).

Travelling by shinkansen is a quintessential Japanese experience, and watching the rituals of the famously quick in-station cleaning operation, the seats automatically turning to face the direction of travel and the attendants bowing on entering and leaving each carriage is not to be missed. An often improbably pretty ekiben (or station bentō, see Bento), which can be bought at all bullet-train terminals, provides essential journey fodder, and picking up an omiyage, or souvenir, from your destination for friends or family is an important part of Japanese travel.

Reservations can be made online or in the ticket offices at stations. When buying tickets at stations, brave the language barrier and speak to someone at a ticket window, rather than relying on ticket machines. Some lines require seat reservations and a complete booking is more easily made in person.

Hokusai
Katsushika Hokusai

This sweeping wave is instantly recognisable as taken from the artist Hokusai's iconic work *The Great Wave off Kanagawa*. Though some might recoil at the reduction of Hokusai's genius to a mere emoji, Hokusai himself was a commercial artist. *The Thirty Six Views of Mount Fuji* series, of which the so-called Great Wave forms part, was excitedly announced in 1831 by one of his publishers as a series of prints in blues, which showcased a new Prussian-indigo dye. Hokusai produced this series of images in his seventies, during a particularly prolific period of activity.

Alongside *The Great Wave off Kanagawa* (the port now subsumed into modern-day Yokohama in Kanagawa Prefecture), Hokusai's *Fine Wind, Clear Morning* is perhaps his other most well-known and loved composition. Part of the same series of views of Fuji, it is indicative of the mountain's enduring hold over the Japanese people. Hokusai produced wood-block prints in a style known as 'floating world pictures' (浮世絵, 'ukiyo-e', in which the 'e' means picture, as in the first sound in 'emoji').

The opening of Japan's borders in the mid-19th century shortly after Hokusai's death led to the dissemination of his work into the West, where he was collected by artists including Monet and Van Gogh. His work would have not just a dramatic impact on Impressionism but a lasting reach into Modernism and Pop Art.

葛飾北斎

Tokyo Tower

Tōkyō tawā

東
京
タ
ワ
ー

At 333m, Tokyo Tower, completed in 1958, is the second tallest structure in Japan, lagging some way behind newcomer Tokyo Skytree, completed in 2012, and currently the second tallest structure in the world.

Much like its inspiration the Eiffel Tower, Tokyo Tower is often used symbolically as an icon of the city. Originally used as the broadcasting tower for state broadcaster NHK, it now broadcasts only analogue television and radio, with digital signals broadcasted from the higher Skytree. The antenna of Tokyo Tower was bent as a result of the March 2011 Tōhoku earthquake disaster, although broadcasting was not affected.

The main viewing platform at 150m is open till 11pm (last admission 10.30pm), and it is said that couples who witness together the tower's lights being extinguished will stay happy. Those in search of such happiness should wait beneath the tower until around midnight. Although the tower is often described as white and red, its actual colours are white and aviation orange, which was dictated by aviation laws for buildings of this height.

While entrance to the Tokyo Tower is cheaper than that to Skytree, visitors on a budget may wish to opt for the 45th floor (202m) observatory of the Tokyo Metropolitan Building (tochō, 都庁) in West Shinjuku, to which entrance is free.

Moyai Statue

moyai zō

モヤイ像

The Moyai Statue is to be found at the South Exit of Tokyo's Shibuya Station. Modelled on the Moai Statues of Easter Island, Tokyo's version was one of many such gifts from the island of Nii-jima, one of the Izu Islands (officially part of Tokyo, despite being over 160km away), and fashioned from the local volcanic *kōga* stone. It was given to Shibuya District in 1980. The statue of Hachikō (see Dog) is by far the more popular Shibuya meeting place but the striking angular Moyai is worthy of a short detour.

Castle

shiro

城

Though hundreds of castles, predominantly from the intense periods of feudal fighting in the 15th and 16th centuries remain in Japan in varying states of repair, there are 12 castles that are denoted Japan's Original Castles, and which retain their original keep.

Perhaps the most famous of these is the dreamlike white Himeji Castle, also known as White Heron Castle, to the west of the region dominated by the historical towns of Kyōto, Kōbe and Ōsaka. The castle is within easy day-trip distance from any of these cities.

While the structure and look of the Japanese castle is quite unique, defensive similarities to Western equivalents such as the impressive moats can be discerned, though the Japanese versions are often filled with vast ornamental carp. At the other end of the spectrum from Himeji's white majesty is brooding black Crow Castle, located in Matsumoto in Nagoya Prefecture on the edge of the Northern Alps. Another of the twelve original castles, Kumamoto Castle, was extensively damaged in the earthquakes on Kyūshū in 2016. Its ongoing restoration is part of the area's concerted drive to bounce back from the misfortune of the earthquakes.

Hot springs

onsen

温
泉

Onsen are a source of enormous pride and enjoyment for the Japanese. The 'rules' for onsen are well documented in all guidebooks, but don't let the idea of rules put you off. After taking your shoes off, buying an entrance ticket (often from a machine) and renting towels (one large, one small), head for the changing room, almost always indicated in English, but it's worth knowing in Japanese, too: 男 for men (always on blue signs); and 女 for women (in red).

From this point on, everything is segregated by gender. Take your clothes off, put into the lockers provided and head through to the shower area with your small towel. Take a stool and shower thoroughly, using the soap and shampoo available and your small towel (if you wish) to scrub until you're really clean ('behind the ears and between the toes' clean). Make sure your body is completely clean of soap suds, give your towel a rinse, too, and head to the pools, which will vary in temperature. The only thing to avoid is putting your small towel in the water. Put it on the side, or on your head for the authentic look. Enjoy the beautiful peace and quiet and don't do anything to impact on it. When you're done, you can dry off using your large towel and change back in the changing room, before heading into mixed-sex areas, where there is often food and drink available.

The onsen logo used in the emoji is pencilled to change in time for the 2020 Olympic and Paralympic Games. Some have previously mistaken it for a sign for a hot drink!

Volcano

kazan

Japan has over 100 active volcanoes, which account for more than 10% of the total number in the world. Mt Fuji (see Mount Fuji) is of course the most well-known, and is constantly monitored for volcanic activity against fears of a potential catastrophe.

Volcano enthusiasts will find much of interest across the country. For example, Sakurajima, in Kagoshima Prefecture, on Kyūshū (see Map of Japan), is one of the most active volcanoes in the world, smoking almost constantly, with minor daily eruptions and, recently, more significant activity (recent research has posited the likelihood of a catastrophic eruption within the next 25 years). It is possible to view the volcano from a variety of viewing platforms.

Closer to Tokyo, many visitors encounter Japanese volcanic life in the town of Hakone, noted for its views of Mt Fuji. The eruption of Mt Hakone over 3,000 years ago created the craterous Owakudani valley, now filled with popular hot springs, although access was restricted in 2015–16 due to an increase in volcanic activity. Eggs are boiled in the sulphuric waters until the shells turn black, and are available for sale. Each egg eaten is said to add seven years to your life, although some say it is not recommended to consume more than two. Whether this is due to a limit on the amount of time that can be added to one's life, or more immediate concerns, is unclear.

Water buffalo

suigyū

The image of carts driven by water buffalo on streets of sand is far from most people's preconceptions of Japan. It is, however, a common sight on the island of Taketomi and is emblematic of the slow tropical vibe that Okinawa offers. Mention Okinawa to 'mainland' Japanese people and you're likely to be greeted by a slightly misty-eyed smile, which befits the magic of these islands.

The Okinawans are famed for their longevity and their diet has been the subject of much scrutiny. There are many uniquely Okinawan dishes, including the intensely bitter melon gōya in a stir-fry called gōya champuru (which often includes the American import of tinned Spam) and braised pork belly known as rafute. Add in the local spirit awamori, sometimes found with a snake in the bottle, and the constant accompaniment of music played on a traditional stringed instrument known as a sanshin and this is geographically and mentally as far from the metropolises of the main island as it's possible to be while remaining on Japanese soil.

With all this on offer, Okinawa is beloved of the Japanese. Many flights land at Naha on the main island (partly dominated by a controversial American army base), from where it would be a missed opportunity not to island hop.

Forest

shinrin

Observing the kanji for a tree (木), a small wood 林 (2 trees) and forest 森 (3 trees) reveals a satisfyingly ordered pattern not matched elsewhere in the Japanese writing system.

Japan's terrain is both highly mountainous and forest-clad. Its forests have been thrust into the international limelight by the concept of 'forest bathing' (森林浴, shinrinyoku). The term emerged in the '80s for the perhaps rather older concept of the restorative physical and mental-health benefits of time spent in woodland nature.

There are likely to be few opponents to the idea that finding time to bask in forest life is more conducive to low stress than standing in the middle of the Shibuya Crossing. Nevertheless, there is undeniably something particularly enchanting about the Japanese forest – perhaps a combination of prized scented trees such as hinoki and hiba (Japanese cypress) and sugi (Japanese cedar); the kami godheads who dwell in the woods and their accompanying shrines (see Shrines) and the opportunity for actual bathing in a woodland onsen.

Yakushima Island, off the southern tip of Kyūshū, is famed for its cedar woodland, and Akasawa in Nagano Prefecture holds some of the country's most celebrated forests. The chance to explore a bamboo forest should also not be overlooked. Those in Arashimaya in the western reaches of Kyōto, and Hokokuji Temple in Kamakura, are two of the more famous examples.

Rugby

ラグビー

ragubī

Rugby's arrival in Japan dates to the turn of the 20th century, when it found popularity in some of Japan's oldest universities. It is one of many sporting rivalries upheld to this day between Tokyo's Waseda and Keio Universities (together called Sōkei and comparable to the rivalry between Oxford and Cambridge). Japanese rugby's real moment in the sun began with a remarkable win for Japan over South Africa in the 2015 Rugby World Cup, and two further wins in the pool-play stages, though Japan failed to qualify for the quarter-finals due to the bonus-points system. The next Rugby World Cup will be held in Japan in autumn 2019. The first Rugby World Cup to be held in Asia, it promises much.

Problems with the Tokyo Olympic Stadium (see Stadium) have prevented its use, but the twelve venues from across Japan (with the majority on the main island of Honshū, three in Kyūshū and one in Hokkaidō) provide an unrivalled opportunity for the sport and its fans to travel and celebrate the game.

The Japanese rugby team, coached by Kiwi Jamie Joseph, are known as the Brave Blossoms and are eyeing a place in the Top 8 and a successful sell-out World Cup across the country.

Football

sakkā

サ
ッ
カ
ー

Football (much more commonly referred to as soccer, or sakkā in its Japanese pronunciation) surged to the fore in Japan in the 1990s. However, the history of Japanese football stretches back over 100 years, from the earliest matches played on naval bases, schools and universities to an Olympic Bronze in 1968, followed by the official creation of the Japan Professional Football League (now known as the J.League) in 1992–3. The league raised the teams from their earlier corporate beginnings to professional teams with a sense of regional identity. At the same time, Japan proceeded from first participating in a Football World Cup in 1998 to co-hosting with Korea in 2002, with the final hosted in Yokohama with the Japanese Emperor in attendance.

Today, the J1 League, the highest in the J-League, comprises 18 teams. The long history of international influence on the Japanese teams is reflected in the team names, from Cerezo Osaka (cerezo is Spanish for cherry tree), to Sanfrecce Hiroshima (a portmanteau of Japanese san 'three' and Italian 'frecce' arrows), to Consadole Sapporo, which takes the Japanese word for people from Hokkaidō 'dōsanko', reverses it and adds the Spanish exclamation *olé* for good measure.

Japan finds itself only in its second decade of a so-called 100-Year Plan for football running to 2092, which aims to expand the Japanese leagues, spread football teams throughout the country and win the FIFA World Cup in this time.

Ski

suki

スキー

Visitors to Japan are often surprised to learn just how mountainous the country is, with the percentage of the country comprising mountain terrain generally given as around 70%. Subsequently, Japan is home to between 400 and 500 ski resorts; no mean feat for a country of its size, though many of these resorts comprise only a few lifts and pistes. Visitors can choose to head either north to Hokkaidō or stay on the main island of Honshū. Niseko and Furano (famed for its spectacular lavender fields in summer) are two of the most popular resorts in Hokkaidō, while those preferring to stay on the main island can choose between the Northern Alps of Nagano Prefecture (including Shiga Kōgen, see Snow monkey) and Niigata Prefecture, which offer resorts within 90 minutes of Tokyo.

First-time Japan skiers and snowboarders will need to get used to the J-Pop accompaniment sometimes piped out onto the slopes. Onsen (see Hot springs) culture could have been invented specifically to ease away cares after a day on the slopes, while other après-ski possibilities naturally vary according to the size and nature of the resort. Hokkaidō resorts in particular can feel very international in season. Ask locals' advice about avoiding the crowds, or consider a tour of some of Japan's 'micro-resorts', which can easily be integrated into the wider exploration of a region.

Martial arts

budō

武
道

The martial-arts uniform, complete with black belt, is known as the keikogi (稽古着). Though often called simply gi outside Japan, detaching this sound from the word in Japanese would make it difficult to understand.

All martial arts, of which Japan has many, have a mental and spiritual dimension that makes their practice a lifetime's work, and the challenge of mastering them has proven the principle draw for many to Japanese culture. Broadly speaking, 'newer' martial arts were introduced to Japan during the Meiji Period. This modernising era, which began in 1868, restored imperial rule and opened up Japanese borders after the period of isolationist closure known as sakoku.

Judō fits into this category, with its founder Jigorō Kanō adapting the practice from the ancient school of jūjutsu (sometime called jujitsu outside Japan). Judō was first introduced as an Olympic sport in 1964 for the first Tokyo Olympics, though women did not participate in judo as a medal sport until 1992. Karate originated in the Ryūkyū Kingdom and came to Japan when this kingdom was annexed as the prefecture of Okinawa in 1879. Kendō, the way of the sword, derives from the more ancient art of kenjutsu and utilises the long bamboo swords known as shinai.

Six major sumō (the Japanese pronunciation, with a short u and long o is the reverse of the Anglicised version) tournaments happen each year, with three in Tokyo (in January, May and September), and the others in Ōsaka (in March), Nagoya (in July) and Fukuoka (in November).

Baseball

yakyū

野
球

The complex dance of American and Japanese culture can be seen in many areas of Japanese society, none more so than in the elevation of baseball in Japan to one of the most popular games in the country.

First introduced in the Meiji Restoration (see Martial Arts), the game was known as both yakyū (literally 'field ball') and bēsubōru until the Second World War when Americanised words were banned and yakyū took prominence. Today, though, both names co-exist.

Robert Whiting's seminal book, *You Gotta Have Wa*, which explores the phenomenon of American players in the Japanese leagues, writes that 'the Japanese found the one-on-one battle between the pitcher and batter similar in psychology to sumo and the martial arts, [involving] split second timing and a special harmony of mental and physical strength'.

The domestic pro game is played by 12 teams split into two leagues of six, the Pacific League and the Central League. The extensive season runs from early April until September, after which the so-called Climax Series determines the Top 3 teams in each league; the winners of each league then meet in the Japan Series in late October. The lively atmosphere and the constant refrain of ouenka (or supporters' songs) attached to individual star players or to the team makes a Japanese baseball match an easy experience to enjoy even if the deep rivalries and intricacies of the game escape you.

Stadium

sutajiamu

ス
タ
ジ
ア
ム

After Tokyo won the bid to host the 2020 Olympic and Paralympic Games, the Japan National Stadium, in the very southern tip of Shinjuku District, generated no shortage of press coverage. It was demolished and plans for its replacement, at the same site, were made to a design by the late Zaha Hadid. Yet public controversy over its perceived cost raged and the plans were shelved, and replaced by a new design by Kengo Kuma.

Two other stadia in Tokyo play home to the capital's two baseball teams – Tokyo Dome, which is also a concert and exhibition venue, for the Yomiuri Giants, and the smaller Jingu Stadium for the Yakult Swallows.

Tokyo Stadium in Chōfu to the west of the city centre is host to the 2019 Rugby World Cup final. The vast 72,000-capacity International Stadium in Yokohama also played host to the 2002 FIFA World Cup final.

Hanafuda

hanafuda

花
札

Hanafuda is the name given to a type of Japanese playing card, where flowers and months replace the standard Western suits. The cards first gained popularity at the end of the 19th century when a company called Nintendo began manufacturing them. Nintendo would go on producing playing cards until the '60s; the rest of its history is well known.

In hanafuda, each month is represented by a different flower. Within the twelve months, there are different combinations of normal cards (one point), ribbon cards (five points), animal cards (ten points) and bright cards (twenty points). The card depicted in the emoji is August's twenty-point card.

The varying combinations depend on the game being played and are not easy to master but, with a little patience and a cheat sheet, it is possible. The cards are available cheaply at 100-yen shops and might provide enough amusement to pass a long journey.

Karaoke

karaoke

カ
ラ
オ
ケ

Karaoke, along with sushi, is perhaps the most notable export of the tech-led Japanese boom of the early 1990s. The word itself is a contraction of the reading *kara* of the character 空 (meaning 'empty') and the Japanisation of the word for orchestra.

It is written カラオケ in the script called katakana used for foreign words (see A note about Japanese language). Those short on time but in need of a karaoke fix may want to make a note as these characters appear stacked in vertical type down the side of many Japanese buildings and for some reason are seldom transliterated into English. Once you've located your chosen venue, the usual form is to book a room at the reception desk, paying per person per hour, sometimes with an expected minimum drinks order. The karaoke machine's menu choices are now often available in English, though a phone in the karaoke box will source help, or more drinks if Dutch courage is needed. The same phone usually rings at the end of a session. As if more encouragement were needed, karaoke machines also sometimes display the calories burned during a particular rendition.

Noh theatre

nō

能

The style of Japanese theatre known as noh is the often cited as the oldest form of theatre in the world, with its origins stretching back to a father/son writer-performer duo in the late 14th century.

Noh plays are performed by a (traditionally) all-male cast, with the leading roles always masked and often appearing sculpture-like and larger than life in multiple layers of clothing. The performances include music, song, dance and dialogue. The plays come from a roster of several hundred, with the most popular inspired by epic stories such as the *Story of Genji* (*Genji Monogatari*). The stages replicate the historically traditional outdoor setting with a roofed, open frame without a curtain. The language used in noh is rarified even to the Japanese and understanding relies on a familiarity with the stories.

Though they are often considered rather hard work for foreigners, tickets for a single act, or traditional summer outdoor performances, provide a lighter experience. The option to take in the last hour of a performance is available at the Kanze Noh Theater, recently relocated to the Ginza Six shopping complex in Tokyo.

The melodramatic style of kabuki theatre developed in a different tradition from noh altogether, with its origins in the 17th century. The white face make-up typical of kabuki is an easy distinguishing factor. Kabuki theatres in major Japanese cities also sell tickets to single parts of the programme.

Calligraphy

shodō

書道

The pictorial Japanese writing system makes the written word an art form in itself. Practised since the advent of writing in Japan (which took its complex characters from Chinese), shodō is still commonly taught and practised in schools today.

The essentials for traditional calligraphy are a brush, an inkstone, inkstick and Japanese calligraphy paper. Though bottled ink is now sometimes used, the true calligrapher grinds their own by pouring a little water into the well of an inkstone and grinding with an inkstick. Shodō takes decades to master and requires both technical ability and a particular state of mind.

The art form has links to Zen Buddhism and requires a clear, calm mind since there is only one chance to commit brush to paper, and the process will mirror your state of mind, revealing the slightest hesitation. The cursive script known as sōsho (草書), which connects its characters and seems to flow vertically down the page, is beautiful to admire and, to the uninitiated eye, hard to read in equal measure.

書道

Anime

anime

ア
ニ
メ

This mark, the only piece of anime culture in the emoji, is drawn on a character's forehead to symbolise anger, or popping veins. The word anime, pronounced a-ni-meh, is used to signify any animation in Japanese, but abroad has become emblematic of Japanese animation alone; likewise, the word manga, which generally denotes anime published in comic-book form.

The two titans in the field are Osamu Tezuka, widely known as the godfather of Japanese manga (himself inspired by Walt Disney) and Hayao Miyazaki, who rose to international fame with *Nausicaa of the Valley of the Wind*, *Spirited Away* and *My Neighbor Totoro*. The latter two films were produced by Studio Ghibli (pronounced Jiburi), which was co-founded by Miyazaki in 1985.

Japanese anime and manga have been credited with a depth of storyline and an emotional intelligence that extends far beyond the traditional reach of the genre for children. Whatever the secret of its international success, which has been hotly pursued by Japanese producers, a whole generation of readers and viewers have come to Japan, its culture and language, predominantly through the influence of anime.

Visitors keen to visit the Ghibli Museum, in the Kichijōji suburb of Tokyo, should read the instructions for ticket purchase carefully in advance of travelling. Tickets sell out quickly before the date of the visit; some are made available through authorised agencies outside of Japan, but the majority are sold through the Loppi machines found in Lawson convenience stores.

Cat

neko

猫

Lucky, cute, relaxing… is there no end to the cat's appeal to the Japanese? The porcelain cat, found across the world as a good-luck talisman in oriental shops and restaurants, originated in Japan. Known as the maneki neko, or beckoning cat, and popular at least since the turn of the 20th century, its origins are disputed, although they are often traced to the story of a cat who beckoned a wealthy man away from a spot that was subsequently struck by lightning. Depending on its colour, the maneki neko can bring good luck in money, love, education or health.

Not dissimilar to the paw of the *maneki neko*, the Japanese hand gesture for ushering someone towards them looks like it has the exact opposite meaning to the unaccustomed eye.

Since the mid-1970s, Hello Kitty has been serious competition for the honour of Japan's most famous feline export. Her full name is Kitty White and, according to creator Sanrio's website, she was born in the 'suburbs of London'. Kitty's can-do attitude and life philosophy of never having too many friends was her ticket to global fame. Now in her 40s, Kitty is a billion-pound business and is a true icon of Japanese kawaii around the world.

Visitors in search of a real feline fix can head to one of the country's many cat cafés. Responsible tourism is encouraged: only support cafés that seem clean, well-maintained, have an emphasis on finding new homes for the cats and allow them space away from customers.

Dog

inu

犬

Pet ownership has long been booming in Japan – since 2003, the numbers of dogs and cats combined have outnumbered children in the country. Space issues in Japanese homes have led the way for the popularity in smaller-sized dogs, which in turn has led to a burgeoning industry of anything from fur stylists to dog yoga.

Perhaps Japan's most famous dog is the faithful Hachikō, who used to greet his master every day at Shibuya Station as he returned home on the train. Though his master had died suddenly, Hachikō still faithfully came to the station hoping to collect him at the appointed time every day for the next 9 years, until his own death in 1935. Hachikō's remarkable loyalty is celebrated by a statue outside Shibuya Station, which also gives its name to one of the station's main exits. Within sight of Shibuya's famous Scramble Crossing, it is one of the most popular meeting places in Tokyo.

Panda

panda

Tokyo's Ueno Zoo is now the proud home to a panda cub named Xiang Xiang, who was born in June 2017 to mother Shin Shin and father Ri Ri. The cub's name was chosen by public ballot, in which over 300,000 people voted, and follows the tradition of names with repeating syllables. The name Xiang Xiang itself comes from the Chinese reading of the character for 'fragrance' 香 (and is pronunced as Shan Shan in Japanese). Xiang Xiang's arrival is particularly poignant as the previous cub born to the same parents died after only 6 days. Her presence will mark a panda boom in the Ueno area of the city, with visitor numbers predicted to soar, and a multi-billion yen boost to local business.

Pandas are also to be found further off the beaten track in the Kansai region in Wakayama Adventure World, where a family of five resides, and in Oji Zoo in Kōbe.

Snow monkey

nihonzaru

The Japanese macaque, or snow monkey, is indigenous to Japan and the image of their bathing in hot springs (see Hot springs) is iconic. The Monkey Park in Jigokudani Valley in Yamanouchi, Nagano Prefecture, is the place to go to find the monkeys huddling for warmth and enjoying the bliss of the hot springs during the snowy months.

A special onsen was constructed for the monkeys after they began to slowly adopt the custom following the behaviour of one particularly inspired simian in the '60s. The monkeys now bathe daily. Humans in search of the same can head for the nearby onsen towns or the ski resorts the prefecture has to offer, including nearby Shiga Kōgen (see Ski).

Snow monkeys can also be seen at the Hakodate City Tropical Botanic Garden, on the southernmost tip of Hokkaidō, a short journey from Hakodate station, often used as an entry point to Hokkaidō by train.

食べ

FOOD
&
DRINK

飲み

Chopsticks

o-hashi

Almost all food of Japanese origin is eaten with chopsticks, and it is of course understood that those who have not grown up with the custom will sometimes experience difficulties or make small etiquette mistakes. The etiquette breaches to particularly avoid are the two funeral customs of leaving chopsticks standing upright in food, particularly rice, and passing food from one set of chopsticks to another. Spearing food with chopsticks is known as sashibashi and is one of several chopstick misdemeanours to have a particular name. Another, mayoibashi, hovering chopsticks indecisively over shared food, suggests that some of the food is better than the rest. Rubbing together the wooden disposable chopsticks, known as waribashi, in a restaurant is also discouraged as it suggests the chopsticks themselves are of poor quality.

However, in general, chopsticks – a bit like dogs – tend to sense fear and the best advice of all is perhaps confidence, while also not trying to attempt the physically impossible. Holding a bowl or plate a little closer to your mouth to eat is perfectly acceptable. For hygiene reasons, if serving from a communal dish, use the serving chopsticks if they are provided or the end of your chopsticks that have not been in your mouth, and, when resting chopsticks but still eating, use the rest known as a hashi-oki, if there is one. Waribashi wrappers can also be folded to fashion a rest.

JAPANEMOJI

Melon

meron

High-end fruit is prized, as near perfect as possible, beautifully packaged and celebrated. Much of the fruit sold in Japan is eye-wateringly expensive and nothing typifies that trend more than the melon.

The cult of Japanese fruit can be traced back to the opening of the Sembikiya fruit store in 1834, which is still in business today, with 14 branches across Tokyo. Sembikiya started life as a discount fruit store, until the wife of one of the founders' descendants had the genius idea of simply making everything more expensive! Slowly, the company began focusing on perfect luxury fruit and started supplying the highest echelons of society. The musk melon became a signature product.

They are now grown with a level of care that extends to putting little hats on top of the fruit to prevent sun damage and they can cost hundreds of pounds to buy. Those wishing to sample the high life without re-mortgaging should head for the Sembikiya Nihonbashi main shop, which has a café showcasing the best of their wares. The jellies and juices on offer in branches also carry slightly more down-to-earth price tags.

Strawberry

ichigo

苺

Perhaps the most stunning of all Japanese fruit, strawberries are often sold in food halls, packaged in boxes like chocolates. As the Japanese for strawberry, ichigo, sounds like the Japanese for one (ichi) and five (go), Strawberry Day is celebrated on either 5 January or 15 January. Strawberry sandwiches are one of the most commonly seen examples of the bizarre phenomenon of fruit sandwiches – crustless white bread, fresh strawberries, custard and/or cream – available anywhere from the humble convenience store to high-end food hall.

Curry rice

karēraisu

カレーライス

As popular in Japan as sushi or ramen, Japanese curry should not be overlooked by visitors to the country just because it doesn't feature on every gourmet checklist. This is known as yōshoku (洋食), or 'Western' food refined to Japanese tastes, the opposite of washoku (和食 – food of Japanese origin), and as such is eaten with a spoon rather than chopsticks. The dish in its most basic form consists of just a thick curry sauce (which – vegetarians beware – usually features small pieces of meat) with rice on the side, and is one of Japan's less visually appealing meals. But forget Instagram, this is food for the end of a busy day, to beat the summer heat with spice or to mop up some of the booze from a big night out. Anything goes for toppings and accompaniments range from katsu to scrambled egg, sausage, squid or vegetables. Cheese is good. When made at home, curry 'roux' blocks are often used, and the sauce has that wonderful nostalgic generic 'curry' taste rather than the complex spicing of other countries' curries. The Coco Ichibanya (CoCo, 壱番屋) chain, with its distinctive yellow signage, is easy to find across Japan and is recommended. Choose your level of spice 1辛, 2辛, 3辛 (ichi-kara, ni-kara, san-kara etc.), or opt for the equivalent scale of sweetness (1甘, ichi-ama etc.).

Cooked rice

gohan

Rice being the staple of the Japanese diet, morning rice (asagohan, 朝ご飯), lunch rice (hirugohan, 昼ご飯) and evening rice (bangohan, 晩ご飯) translate as breakfast, lunch and dinner, respectively. Restaurant-portion sizes are often indicated by the size of rice bowl, with ōmori (大盛り, literally 'big bowl') a universally available option for the hungry diner.

Donburi is the name given to rice bowls topped with any number of ingredients with gyūdon (beef) or butadon (pork) among the most popular. Add toppings such as kimchi, spring onions or cheese and tabasco at chains such as Sukiya or Yoshinoya. Eel over rice, known as unadon, is popular and also found at specialist unagi restaurants at a higher price tag.

A soup called ochazuke (お茶漬け) is made from rice covered in green tea, often flavoured with the preserved sour plum known as umeboshi or salted salmon, with strips of seaweed, and is excellent as comfort food and when feeling unwell.

Ramen

rāmen

Ramen is always there for you, even in the small hours, cheap, hot and filling.

Many Japanese people will acknowledge that ramen is Chinese in origin, while at the same time claiming this soul food as their own national sustenance. Ramen comes in a bewildering number of permutations, with menus often making the major delineation by type of base – salt (shio), soy sauce (shōyu) or miso. These bases combine with broths of kelp (kombu), bonito flakes (katsuobushi), chicken or pork bone (tonkotsu) and toppings too varied to list, but include chāshū pork slices, sheets of nori, spring onion and egg, with regional variations such as the corn and butter on offer in Hokkaidō.

The normal order in a ramen shop (and they are definitely shops ('ramen-ya' – ya meaning shop) and not restaurants in Japanese) is to pay at a machine and take a ticket; the server will sometimes ask you how rich/fatty you'd like the soup and how you'd like the noodles cooked (the easiest answer to both is 'futsū' – regular). The Chinese dumplings known as gyōza (see page 110) are a popular side order. Not only do most regions have their own style of ramen, but people will also claim allegiance to the style of individual restaurants. Slurp at will and marvel at the heat at which some diners can consume the broth at speed.

Sushi
o-sushi

'Sushi' refers to anything prepared with vinegared rice, rather than meaning raw fish. Eat it with fingers or chopsticks, but always in one mouthful. The most commonly enjoyed type is nigirizushi (the word sushi becomes zushi in compound words) as depicted in the emoji. Nigirizushi should be turned so that the fish, rather than the rice, is lightly dipped into soy sauce, as otherwise the rice will soak up too much soy and break down. It is polite to pour just enough soy sauce into your dish, great lakes are considered potentially wasteful.

Makizushi are sushi rolls with nori (seaweed) on the outside, oshizushi is a type of sushi pressed into a rectangular box that is a speciality of Ōsaka, and gunkan-maki are the boat shapes that often hold fish roe, or sea urchin. Chirashizushi showcases a range of ingredients beautifully arranged on top of rice.

Top sushi restaurants seat only a handful of customers where the experienced chef (板前, ita-mae) presides over the counter – book these in advance. At the cheaper end of the spectrum are kaitenzushi (回転寿司); here, help yourself to price-coded plates from the revolving conveyor belt or shout your order out to the chefs in the centre. As in all sushi restaurants, only sushi is ordered from the chefs; drinks and other items are ordered from waiting staff. Another budget-friendly option is to head to a depachika (the basement food hall in large department stores), where items are discounted towards the end of the day.

Bento

o-bentō

お
弁
当

Boxed meals known as bentō are prepared by parents for their children to take to school, or are taken to work, eaten on picnics, planes or trains, bought in department-store food halls, convenience stores, specialist shops, or in restaurants. They are compartmentalised and often contain rice and pickled vegetables. You'll find a range of colours, textures and styles of cooking, which showcase the balance of flavours that is important to the Japanese – the choice is endless.

The bentō pictured in the emoji contains a single pickled sour Japanese plum (umeboshi, 梅干し) in the centre of the rice, which is a style of bentō known as 'hinomaru', the name of the Japanese flag.

Kitchenware sections in Japanese department stores feature a huge variety of bentō boxes, from the sleekly modern to the cutesy kawaii. Along with the chopsticks often sold nearby, they make excellent souvenirs or gifts. Parents may also find inspiration in the innovative goods on hand designed to make lunchboxes more enticing.

Preparing for a train journey or short flight by seeking out the finest bentō in the airport or station will leave you feeling well-prepared, and fighting a desire not felt since school coach trips to eat it in its entirety within minutes of departure.

Delicious

oishii

お
い
し
い

In a country where communication can be hard-going, one word beyond the pleasantries can be a saviour: *oishii* or delicious (when written with kanji as 美味しい, the meaning is literally 'beautiful taste').

A simple word of appreciation goes a long way, and saying oishii (Oishii des(u) or 'it's delicious', with the verb, is more polite) after a first mouthful will be much appreciated.

Oishi-sō is also frequently used when looking at food and means 'it looks delicious.' This quiet appreciation of food is important. The word Itadakimas(u), a polite form of the verb to receive, is said before eating, and is a moment to acknowledge both the ingredients and those that have prepared them rather than a celebratory, 'Bon appetit!' The polite way to thank those who have bought, prepared or cooked you a meal is to say, 'go-chisō-sama deshita'; the openness of Japanese kitchens normally allows you to say this when leaving a restaurant.

Chicken

toriniku

Yakitori (焼き鳥, literally 'grilled chicken') is the best way to sample chicken in Japan and indeed can often produce an introduction to parts of a chicken you've never before dreamed of eating.

Yakitori joints are drinking establishments, the air often thick with the smell of charcoal and cigarette smoke. Parts of the chicken are put onto small skewers and grilled over open charcoal. It is usually possible to sit at the counter, where the chef will hand plates of skewers directly to you. More everyday items include chicken thigh, breast, meatballs (tsukune), and chicken and spring onion (negima).

Anything goes for more adventurous options, including cartilage, liver, gizzard, heart and tail. It's perfectly possible to skip all of these but those appalled by such a list may be better served by prioritising something else. Other vegetable options are often served, such as shiitake, gingko nut and enoki mushrooms wrapped in bacon. Discard your used skewers in the pots provided. Yakitori is also commonly on offer in izakayas (see Izakaya lantern).

Meat

o-niku

Sukiyaki and shabu shabu are two Japanese styles of cooking meat well worth seeking out. The thinly sliced raw meat is brought to the table or counter and, in sukiyaki, cooked in a sweetened hot pot of soy sauce and mirin alongside vegetables and tofu before being dipped in raw egg and eaten. Shabu shabu is named after the sound of swishing the meat, each piece at a time, in a hot pot enriched with kombu (kelp), before being dipped in sauce.

Shabu shabu and sukiyaki (in certain regions) are served with beef and pork, pork being the most commonly consumed meat in Japan. One of the finest Japanese pork dishes to savour is tonkatsu (豚カツ), a breaded pork cutlet often served in a set meal with a mound of raw, finely shredded cabbage, a sweet brown sauce, and mustard, accompanied by rice, pickles and miso soup.

Wagyū (和牛, literally Japanese cow) is prized and instantly recognisable for its incredible marbled fat. The fat breaks down at low temperatures, coating the meat in its juices and creating a flavour quite unlike any other beef in the world.

Perhaps the finest showcase for Japanese beef is, ironically, in the cuisine of Korean origin known as yakiniku (焼肉), where your chosen cuts of meat are barbecued at the table. The most popular yakiniku restaurants book up well ahead of time. (Note: the restaurant chain Sukiya, seen across Japan, serves gyūdon, see Cooked rice, not sukiyaki.)

Onigiri

onigiri

おにぎり

Sushi is not available in convenience stores, but the un-vinegared onigiri may perhaps be considered its workaday cousin. Onigiri are simply rice balls, usually formed into triangles or rounds when sold commercially, but also commonly shaped into any variety of novelty forms for children's lunchboxes (see Bento). As they are often surrounded entirely by a sheet of seaweed (nori, 海苔) and then rice, their fillings are usually concealed and as such can represent Russian roulette to the non-reader of Japanese. Some convenience stores have now started labelling their flavours in English, too. Common fillings include sour pickled plum (umeboshi, 梅干し), spicy fish roe (mentaiko, 明太子) and Western-inspired options such as tuna mayo and fried chicken. To unwrap onigiri, find the labels 1, 2 and 3 on the wrapper, peeling the central strip first, followed by the edges, rewrapping the seaweed around the rice as it comes away from the plastic.

Shrimp tempura

ebi tenpura

エ
ビ
天
ぷ
ら

The deep-frying of seafood or vegetables in batter known as tempura is a precision art, introduced to Japan via the Portuguese in the 16th century. Often served over rice when it is called tendon (天丼) or with soba or udon noodles, tempura is such an art that it is worth seeking out a restaurant famed for its skill. Tempura is normally served with a dipping sauce called tsuyu (汁), into which you can mix the grated daikon or ginger that comes as an accompaniment, although salt is sometimes offered as an alternative. Eat hot and fresh.

Octopus

tako

た
こ

Perhaps the most perennially popular Japanese street food are the fried octopus balls known as takoyaki. A delicious textural contrast between soft hot batter and the bite of a central piece of octopus, covered in sweet-savoury sauce, mayonnaise, aonori seaweed powder and the essential Japanese ingredient of katsuobushi, the wonderfully savoury flakes of dried bonito, that provides a base note to many Japanese dishes.

If the constituent parts of takoyaki sound unfamiliar, the queues of hungry eaters in front of takoyaki stalls ought to convert the sceptical. They are made in a distinctive hot pan of numerous spherical moulds, turned with speed and dexterity by the vendors. Takoyaki are available across Japan but are claimed as a local dish in Ōsaka, where visitors to Universal Studios can also visit the Takoyaki Museum. Takoyaki are also a popular snack at baseball matches or other sporting events.

Squid

ika

イ
カ

Japanese squid have made a global splash (of sorts) in a viral Internet video of the so-called 'dancing squid dish', in which a very recently killed squid's nerves are stimulated by the addition of soy sauce, where the sodium chloride in the soy makes its tentacles appear to dance. It has become associated with various towns on Hokkaidō and, while undeniably a spectacle, it's certainly more widely consumed as a video by YouTube junkies than as a Japanese meal.

Squid is commonly eaten in Japan as nigiri sushi or tempura, but it is perhaps as the dried squid known as surume or atarime that it is most commonly encountered. This phenomenally chewy snack is available in every convenience store, or on every bullet train drinks trolley, and is thought of as a drinking snack or o-tsumami, particularly suited to beer. Persimmon-seed-shaped rice crackers mixed with peanuts (known as Kaki-pī, see Senbei) are another famous example, as is chītara (or cheese-tara), a stick of cheese between two thin layers of minced fish.

Fox

kitsune

き
つ
ね

The fox – kitsune in Japanese – has multiple symbolic associations in the country's folklore. They can be largely divided into the good but mischievous, and the malevolent and, in yōkai folklore (see Tengu), they are particularly associated with their ability to shape-shift into human form. In the Shintō faith (see Shrine), the kitsune is the messenger of Inari, the deity of the rice harvest, and statues of the fox can be seen at most Inari shrines, famous for their long paths of red torii, with the spectacular Fushimi Inari-taisha in Kyōto being the most famous example.

The messenger-fox's favourite food was said to be the slice of fried tofu known as aburaage, which has given rise to a popular dish known as kitsune udon ('the fox udon') in which udon noodles in a sweetened dashi broth lie underneath a slice of aburaage. The sweet chewy tofu is delicious and quite different from the common perception of this (sometimes welcomingly) bland ingredient. When aburaage are opened and their pockets filled with seasoned sushi rice, these are known as inari sushi (or inarizushi). The 'cousin' of kitsune udon is tanuki udon (or 'raccoon udon') and has crunchy pieces of deep-fried tempura (known as tenkasu) as a topping in place of the aburaage.

Rice cracker

senbei

煎
餅

Toasted Japanese rice crackers are available in a number of varieties, most often savoury and painted with soy sauce (or a sweetened sauce of soy and mirin) as they are baked, or less commonly in a sweet version. The emoji shows a sheet of nori (seaweed) wrapped around the cracker; this is also sometimes found in a version where the nori has been shredded and mixed into the dough before baking.

The mixed rice cracker pieces that are now popular all over the world are known as arare ('hailstones'). The crescent-moon-shaped senbei are known as kaki no tane (柿の種, literally 'persimmon seeds' after their shape) and when mixed with peanuts make a snack that goes well with beer called kaki-pī (柿ピー). Senbei and green tea is what is commonly offered to visitors to a Japanese home. You can still see senbei being made and baked over charcoal in older districts, and buy and eat them warm.

Roasted sweet potato

yaki-imo

焼き
き
い
も

A popular snack commonly sold as the cold sets in, the roasted sweet potato and its street vendors inspire nostalgia. Selling from a cart, or now more commonly from the back of a small van, sweet-potato sellers announce themselves with a song: 'Yaki-imo, ishiyaki-imo!' ('Baked sweet potato, stone-baked sweet potato!'). They are generally eaten just as they are without condiments.

Purple-flesh varieties of sweet potato, known generally as murasaki imo, are particularly common in Okinawa, and are often used to make desserts, including a purple soft-serve ice cream and a cheesecake.

Dango

dango

The chewy Japanese snack/dessert known as dango exists in various incarnations. All are based on a dough made from rice flour formed into small dumplings. The emoji depicts three-colour dango, or sanshoku dango (三色団子), which are particularly associated with sakura season (see Cherry blossom) or Girls' Day (see Japanese dolls), though they are now available all year round and often seen in convenience stores.

Mitarashi dango have a base of plain white dango, often finished under the grill or on open charcoal, covered in a salty-sweet soy sauce. Pure white unadorned dango are associated with tsukimi (see Moon viewing). A smaller white version of dango known as shiratama (白玉, literally white spheres) are commonly found in desserts, and often served with ice cream and a black molasses syrup known as kuromitsu and a roasted-soya-bean flour called kinako, or with kuromitsu, red bean paste, fruit, and agar jelly in a summer dessert called anmitsu. The shiratama are a textural foil and appreciating their blandness takes a slight change of mindset for a Western palette. Making dango differs from the other common Japanese glutinous rice dessert mochi in starting with rice flour; the process of making mochi begins with the rice itself.

Cucumber

kyūri

きゅうり

The Japanese for cucumber is kyūri, but the popular cucumber sushi rolls are known universally as kappa maki, after Kappa, perhaps the Japanese equivalent of Nessie – a malevolent water-dwelling character of folklore, whose favourite food is cucumber.

Fish cake

narutomaki

なると巻き

Another emoji widely used for a variety of purposes, this in fact represents narutomaki, a type of processed fish cake commonly used as a topping for ramen or soba, possibly more for its decorative values than its taste, which is quite mild. Its name comes from the whirlpools off the coast of Naruto, on Shikoku Island.

Gyōza

Gyōza

餃
子

Gyōza are the Japanese equivalent of the traditional Chinese jiaozi dumpling. They can be served as yaki-gyōza (焼き餃子) where they are fried (the steam-fry method of cooking in itself is worth observing), which creates a lace-like crust; or the simpler dish of sui-gyoza (水餃子), where they are boiled. They are a common accompaniment to ramen; specialty gyōza bars also exist. The most usual meat in the filling is pork; garlic and the garlic chive known as nira are often also used.

Blowfish

fugu

Fugu – puffer or blowfish in English – is well known as being lethally poisonous unless properly prepared. The jeopardy involved has made fugu infamous and there are various dedicated restaurants where you can go to roll the dice. As chefs require three years training before being permitted to serve the fish, eating fugu in a restaurant is the only safe bet. It is amateur domestic preparation that has led to the majority of deaths. The fish is served as sashimi or in a hotpot. Serving the liver, which is one of the most toxic parts of the fish, is now banned in restaurants. There are recorded cases where chefs have been caught flouncing this rule, which have sometimes resulted in customers being hospitalised. The price is high, and the taste generally considered to be unremarkable. You, as they say, do the math.

Fries

furaido poteto

フライドポテト

McDonald's in Japan, or Makudonarudo (マクドナルド) , recently had a turbulent time, with a series of food-safety scandals seriously damaging its reputation. With changes including a new CEO, a co-promotion with Pokémon Go and a new speciality – chocolate sauce on fries! – things suddenly started to look up for McDonald's. In a country as receptive as Japan to bizarre and photographic food stunts, the McChoco Potato struck just the right note.

A plate of fries, without the chocolate sauce, is as essential to an izakaya spread (see izakaya lantern) as homegrown Japanese cuisine and popular hybrids like deep-fried karaage chicken. The occasional sight of a single fry being eaten with chopsticks in an izakaya is the very model of Japanese restraint.

Candy

kyandi

The Japanisation 'kyandi' is indicative of the American influence over snack and convenience-store culture, whereas 'sweets' (suwītsu, スウィーツ) denotes something closer to patisserie. Raiding a convenience store or 100-yen shop (see Yen and Convenience store) for weird and wonderful candy is a Japan essential. Muscat grape is a commonly found flavour, along with the usual suspects in unusual packages. If you are a non-reader of Japanese whose face suddenly feels a little tighter, you may have unwittingly bought a packet of candy that contains collagen (see Beauty).

Little chocolate bamboo shoots or mushrooms are cute and popular; along with the chocolate-covered biscuit sticks called Pocky, which practically have a cult following and are increasingly easy to find outside Japan.

Weird and wonderful flavours of KitKat, such as musk melon, sake, butter or cheesecake (or even some flavours like crème brûlée, which can be baked in the oven) can be found in some convenience stores, but the true devotee should head to a KitKat-branded concession in a department store or the special 'luxury' KitKat store in Ginza in Tokyo. The Japanese kittokatto sounds like 'kitto katsu', which translates as 'you will certainly win', making KitKats a traditional sweet to give for good luck.

Chocolate

chokorēto

チョコレート

In common with the rest of the world, Valentine's Day is chocolate's big moment in the Japanese calendar. However, it comes with a twist – that, come 14 February, only women give chocolate to men, and not vice versa. One version of the origins of this tradition is that it was a simple mistranslation of an American advertisement.

Whatever its origin, the chocolate companies' marketing departments had successfully established the tradition by the 1960s, and it is now big business. The complexities of Japanese society are represented in the different types of chocolate given, with special, homemade or expensive chocolates for a loved one, chocolates given as a token to male co-workers or classmates, and those given by women to their female friends.

A savvy marketing company tried to buck the trend recently with the introduction of 'gyaku' (reverse) chocolates for men to give to women on Valentine's Day. However, the real opportunity to repay the gift, comes exactly a month later on White Day, 14 March. What began in the '70s as Marshmallow Day now extends to white chocolate, lingerie or any other present of the man's choosing. It is often said that when reciprocating romantic Valentine's Day chocolates, the man is expected to double or triple the value of the gift he received.

Shaved ice

kakigōri

Kakigōri is *the* essential Japanese summer treat. It is made by shaving ice from a larger block, either by hand, or more commonly by machine, to the consistency of fresh snow. The ice is then covered with syrup, flavourings, toppings and often condensed milk to sweeten. Flavours are as abundant as varieties of ice cream, and include strawberry, lemon, melon, mango (with fresh fruit), Blue Hawaii (a bright-blue soda flavour) or matcha, often topped with matcha powder and red adzuki beans. The Japanese taste for beans with ice, which gives them a toffee-like texture, has to be acquired. While kakigōri has long been popular in Japan, a recent craze has seen hour-long queues snake out of the door of the most popular shops.

Shirokuma (literally 'polar bear', 白くま) is a delicious variety of kakigōri flavoured with condensed milk and topped with red beans, pineapple, mandarin and other fruits. A variety of this is sold in tubs in most convenience stores for those willing to trade a queue for a less-authentic experience.

Kakigōri has a standardised sign used across Japan at point-of-sale. Look for a red Japanese symbol for ice 氷, with blue waves lapping underneath.

Oden

oden

お
で
ん

This much-misused emoji is the symbol of oden, a classic winter dish. Any number of ingredients – including hard-boiled egg, fishcakes, fried tofu, daikon and konnyaku (a chewy gelantinous paste made from the root of a plant and known as shirataki in its calorie-free noodle form) are simmered in hot dashi (Japanese stock). Often first encountered in the slightly spooky version that sits at till points in convenience stores in winter, it's also well worth seeking out a speciality oden restaurant, where your chosen ingredients can be selected from the pots in which they simmer and will be served with a little of the stock ladled over the top and hot mustard on the side.

Sake
nihonshu

日
本
酒

Sake, or politely o-sake, is the Japanese for all alcohol and written 酒. What countries outside of Japan call sake is called nihon-shu (日本酒, Japanese alcohol). For an introduction to nihonshu, find a sake shop with English-speaking staff or a restaurant with a sake sommelier.

There are over 1,200 nihonshu breweries in Japan, all working with the same ingredients of rice, water, yeast and a mould grown on white rice called kōji. Premium sake is graded, with Junmai Daiginjō being the 'highest' grade (indicating that the grains have been milled to 50% of their weight). Milling removes the fats and proteins from the outer layer of the grain, which impact on the final flavour.

Sake is usually aged for around 6 months, at low temperatures. It will not keep well unrefrigerated for much longer periods. Sake is served in measures, called gō; the ichigō (一合) measure equals 180ml and is enough for one serving or a modest serving to share. A sake flask, known as a tokkuri, often comes in ichigō (1-gō) or nigō (2-gō) sizes, the small cups are called o-choko. Sake is sometimes (in an informal setting) poured into your glass overflowing into a wooden box (or masu) as a gesture of hospitality. The contents of the masu can be poured back into your glass when there is room.

Very generally speaking, sake is best served lightly chilled. Some sake may be enjoyed gently warmed in winter.

Wine

wain

ワ
イ
ン

Wine lovers in Japan may find the most obvious choices to be wine found in convenience stores, which in most cases would be best avoided in favour of beer or sake, or expensive imported wine in depachika (the basement food hall in large department stores). But it is worth hunting for Japanese wines instead.

The kōshū grape is perhaps the country's most famous indigenous variety and is grown in Yamanashi Prefecture (containing the foothills of Mount Fuji), which contains 80 wineries. It produces a clean, pale, fresh white wine, often naturally low in alcohol.

The Delaware grape, also popular in Japan, produces slightly sweeter, sometimes sparkling varieties.

Japanese wine is just unusual enough to make hunting out the best a challenge, while the scale of production is small enough to build up a base of knowledge in a relatively short amount of time.

Kanpai

Kanpai

乾
杯

Compared to the humble spirit in which Itadakimasu is often said before eating, kanpai is, in everyday life, a hearty, 'Cheers!'

When written in kanji, the meaning 'dry cup' reveals itself, though it no longer denotes a necessity to drain your glass. Saying kanpai is pretty well obligatory and people wait to drink until everyone has said it; beer is often the first drink ordered by everyone to keep this process simple. Japanese drinking etiquette denotes that you pour a drink for your drinking partner(s) and they for you.

The Japanese culture of nomikai (飲み会) sees the workplace move from the office to the bar or izakaya. This is an etiquette black hole, considered to be something of a hornets' nest, where it is wise to be attentive to topping up your superiors' drinks and drunkenness is permissible, though much behaviour that accompanies drunkenness would be considered highly inappropriate.

The expense of taxis and relative distance of most homes in the suburbs means that many drinking sessions end with a sprint for the last train.

The sight of incredibly drunk Japanese businessmen at train stations or asleep on trains is, therefore, not uncommon.

Japanese tea

o-cha

お茶

O-cha is the catch-all name for Japanese tea; it always denotes a type of green tea, rather than kōcha (紅茶), which is black tea. Regular green tea is graded by the quality of the leaf: gyokuro is the highest grade, with its leaves protected from the sun during growth, followed by kabusecha, sencha then bancha.

Roasted green-tea leaves make a tea called hōjicha, while genmaicha combines green-tea leaves with toasted brown rice. The dustier leaves left over in green-tea production are known as konacha. You'll find this in sushi restaurants, offered free of charge by self-service hot taps around the counter.

Konacha is different from the powdered green tea known as matcha (抹茶), which is graded according to the leaves from which it is milled. Matcha can be found in sponge cakes, layered crepe cakes, doughnuts and cookies, as well as KitKats and other chocolate bars.

Matcha is used in the famous tea ceremony known as sadō (茶道, also pronounced chadō, or known as cha-no-yu, 茶の湯), which has its roots in Buddhism. It is performed in a special tea room, or separate tea house, and is said to embody the principle of wabi sabi by finding beauty in imperfection, recognising the relative emptiness of the tea room and celebrating transience in the ripples in the matcha as it is whisked with the distinctive spider-like whisk. Light Japanese sweets or sometimes a light kaiseki meal are served before the tea.

Resources

Donny Kimball
https://donnykimball.com
A man on a mission to get travellers off the beaten track. There is much to find here for those looking to avoid the traditional Tokyo and Kyoto itinerary of a first visit to Japan.

Emojipedia®
https://emojipedia.org
The essential online guide to all things emoji.

Food Sake Tokyo
https://foodsakeTokyo.com
Authoritative blog on all aspects of Japanese food and drink. The author Yukari Sakamoto has also published a guide to Japanese eating and drinking and has a lively Twitter feed.

Hyperdia.com
For train timetables for the different Japan Rail subsidiaries.

Japan Guide
https://www.japan-guide.com
Very useful one-stop resource for information on all areas of Japanese life, particularly strong on travel and culture.

Jinja Honcho Association of Shinto Shrines
http://www.jinjahoncho.or.jp/en/
Further reading on shrine etiquette and the Shinto faith.

Surviving in Japan (without much Japanese)
http://www.survivingnjapan.com
Forensically detailed blog for the minutiae of everyday life in Japan; this is where to go for instructions when you can't understand the controls of your A/C remote control, or need to print out something in a convenience store.

Television
Terrace House (Netflix)
A rare opportunity to watch Japanese television with English subtitles, this reality-TV show is now produced by Netflix. The show observes 6 young people living together in a house in various locations in Japan, or (for one series) in Hawaii. It is the family of presenter-commentators and their warmth, humour and insights, that make the show.
Midnight Diner (Netflix)
The most recent series of this show is also available on Netflix and takes place late at night in a fictional izakaya in Tokyo. Each episode generally focuses on one customer and their requested dish.

The Japan Times
https://www.japantimes.co.jp
The primary English-language newspaper in Japan. An essential source of news, comment and features on Japanese life.

Time Out Tokyo
https://www.timeout.com/Tokyo
Time Out's site is an excellent source for listings of all sorts in the capital, as well as restaurant reviews. The bimonthly printed edition is available for free at numerous points in the city, as are useful *Things to Do in…* area guides.

Tokyo Cheapo
https://tokyocheapo.com
Excellent advice for travelling in Tokyo and beyond on a budget.

Further reading

Non-fiction

Kimiko Barber, The Japanese Kitchen
(Kyle Books, 2004)
An authoritative guide to the Japanese kitchen; an essential resource for a deeper understanding of Japanese cooking and ingredients.

Brian Bocking, A Popular Dictionary of Shinto
(Curzon Press, 1995; out of print)
A definitive dictionary of the Japanese Shinto faith and its shrines.

Will Ferguson, Hokkaido Highway Blues
(Canongate, 2001)
A Japanese-travel hitchhiking odyssey following the spread of the cherry blossom from south to north.

Makiko Sano, Shoku Iku: Japanese Conscious Eating for a Long and Healthy Life
(Quadrille, 2015)
An excellent entry point to innovative and simple modern Japanese cooking and the Japanese philosophy of food.

Robert Twigger, Angry White Pyjamas
(Phoenix, 1997)
One man's quest to train in the martial art of Aikido on the intensive course taken by the Japanese riot police.

Robert Whiting, You Gotta Have Wa
(Viking, 1989)
Classic account of the culture clash between American and Japanese baseball.

Fiction

What follows is intended only as a very small sample of the breadth of Japanese fiction available in translation.

Yusanari Kawabata, Snow Country
(Penguin Classics, 2011; originally published in Japanese in 1956)
Delicate love story of a young man who travels from Tokyo to the mountains of West Japan to meet a geisha.

Hiromi Kawakami, Strange Weather in Tokyo
(Portobello, 2014; originally published in Japanese in 2012)
A recent international success, a tale of an affair between a woman and one of her former teachers, against the backdrop of the changing seasons in the capital.

Yukio Mishima, The Sailor Who Fell From Grace With the Sea
(Vintage, 1999; originally published in Japanese in 1963)
Allegorical novel of innocence lost and retribution among a group of thirteen-year-old boys; it is said to have inspired David Bowie.

Haruki Murakami, Norwegian Wood
(Vintage, 2000; originally published in Japanese in 1983)
An excellent book to use as an entry point to Japan's most celebrated literary export, a story of love and loss in the 1960s. The author's non-fiction works *Underground* and *After the Quake* also provide insight into Japanese society *in extremis*.

Ryu Murakami, Coin Locker Babies
(Pushkin Press, 2013; originally published in Japanese in 1980)
Offbeat postmodern novel by the lesser-known Murakami, the parallel lives of two brothers abandoned in Tokyo coin lockers.

A note about Japanese language

All Japanese words are made up of units of sound (called mora) that are themselves either a single vowel, or a consonantal sound plus a vowel. A single *n* sound is the exception. Examples of these units might be the sounds *ho, ma, su, da, to, shi, o, go, kyo* etc. Any Japanese word will fit into this pattern. For example, sushi = *su* + *shi*, sake = *sa* + *ke*. Foreign words and names that come into Japanese have to be adapted to fit this phonetic system, so hotel becomes hoteru (*ho* + *te* + *ru*), wine becomes wain (*wa* + *i* + *n*).

The length of vowels in Japanese is important. Long vowels are marked in this book with a bar over the top – ō for long o, and ū for long u. The length of a vowel can completely change the meaning of a word. Other vowels tend to be shorter than English so wasabi is wa-sa-bi not wasaaaabi; sushi is su-shi, not sooshi. Tokyo has two long vowels Tōkyō, which are not indicated in this book, where Tokyo appears with its normal English spelling.

Japanese has two writing systems, which can both represent all of the sounds described. The script known as **hiragana** is generally used for words of Japanese origin and word endings, and the script called **katakana** is used for foreign words, foreign names, and sometime plants and animals. Neither script can be learnt overnight but with a few concerted study sessions and some practice, they can be mastered. Learning katakana is generally considered the slightly harder of the two but bears dividends more quickly as all loan words into Japanese become instantly readable.

The real complexity of written Japanese lies in the characters of Chinese origin called **kanji**. In words written with kanji, the kanji contain the word's central meaning; grammatical extras such as verb endings are added in hiragana. To complicate matters further, most kanji have at least two 'readings' – i.e. can be pronounced in at least two different ways: one a native

Japanese pronunciation; the other closer to the original Chinese pronunciation. Learning to write and correctly pronounce kanji can take a lifetime for the learner of Japanese as a foreign language. A reliance on smartphones and computers to write kanji increasingly causes problems even for the Japanese with rarer and more complex characters.

The good news (of sorts) is that you can recognise the meaning of kanji without knowing how to pronounce them. The most useful at-a-glance characters to know are:

円　yen
人　person
出　going out (used with 口 to mean exit)
入　coming in (used with 口 to mean entrance)
入　is also used to represent 'on', with 切 used for 'off'
上　up
下　down
駅　station
空　empty/vacant
満　full
禁　forbidden
止　stop (written on roads… and toilets)

It is undeniably overwhelming, but even by memorising the shape of one or two characters above, or the name of a nearby metro, you'll be surprised when you start to see the character recurring elsewhere.

The Japanese language has many important levels of politeness, the simplest of which is an honorific prefix o- or go-. This is added to the start of many words to indicate a respect for the topic and is given in translations in this book – for example, o-sushi for sushi and o-sake for alcohol.

Acknowledgements

A huge thank you:
To my editor Laura Higginson, and to Sophie Yamamoto for her care and creativity in making this book so beautiful. To Rae Shirvington for all her support over the years and to Alice Latham. To Kyoko Tachibana for copy editing. To Jon Elek and Rosa Schierenberg at United Agents.

Love and thanks to my parents for everything, and for instilling in me my love of languages, and to my sister Harriet, her husband Tunde and my beautiful nephew Griffin. To my friends, especially Vicki Scott & Chrissy Sweeney, and James & Laura Waddilove, who were there at the very beginning of my Japan obsession; ten years later, this book is dedicated to your children with love. To Ellie Rankine, Amelia Evans, Hannah Cowie & Kelly Ellis for always being there; Luthfa Begum who started it all off and Annie Stradling who first came to Japan with me.

To Willy Ballmann, Phyllis Chia and Jonathan Savoie for helping me find my feet in Tokyo. Lastly, to everyone who has taught me Japanese, in London and in Tokyo, for all your patience and good humour. There is undoubtedly something each of you has taught me in here.

10 9 8 7 6 5 4 3 2 1

Published in 2019 by Pop Press
an imprint of Ebury Publishing,

20 Vauxhall Bridge Road,
London SW1V 2SA

Pop Press is part of the Penguin Random House group of companies whose addresses can be found at global.penguinrandomhouse.com

Penguin Random House UK

First published by Pop Press in 2019

www.penguin.co.uk

A CIP catalogue record for this book is available from the British Library

ISBN 978 1 785 0 3989 8

Colour origination by BORN Ltd
Printed and bound in China by Toppan Leefung

Design and illustrations: maru studio

MIX
Paper from responsible sources
FSC
www.fsc.org
FSC® C018179

Penguin Random House is committed to a sustainable future for our business, our readers and our planet. This book is made from Forest Stewardship Council® certified paper.